Volume 1 _____ Baja, Mexico.

AMBR°SIA

Adam Goldberg
Editor in Chief

Daniela Velasco
Creative Director

Elyssa Goldberg
Executive Editor

John Surico
Copy Editor

Bonjwing Lee
Copy Editor

The best way to come to know a place and its food is to arrive hungry, ask questions, and eat as the locals do—especially when those locals are a region's great chefs. Welcome to *Ambrosia*, a new print magazine where interviews with chefs, and the recipes they supply, help guide you through some of the world's most compelling eating destinations.

For *Ambrosia's* first issue, we traveled 750 miles, south-to-north, along Mexico's lesser-known west coast, the Baja Peninsula, to speak with seaside *marisqueros* and internationally acclaimed chefs to bring you a taste of what makes the region's cuisine so vibrant.

Diversity is the cornerstone of Baja. Home to two of Mexico's newest states, Baja California to the north and Baja California Sur to the south, Baja has, over the last several decades, welcomed with open arms transplants hailing from countries as far away as China and as nearby as mainland Mexico. Today, the various heritages of Baja's residents, and the countless stories, recipes, and cooking techniques they brought with them, combine to create a dynamic food culture distinctive to the peninsula.

In Tijuana, chefs like Javier Plascencia cook to help rebrand the food-rich, yet international press-maligned city. On the coast in Ensenada, the vivacious Sabina Bandera piles abundant sea urchin atop crunchy *tostadas* at her no-tables-allowed roadside stand. And just twenty miles inland in Mexico's wine country, Valle de Guadalupe, a Mediterranean climate and nearby fertile waters inspire the local vegetable and fresh fish-driven cuisine of chefs like Drew Deckman and Diego Hernández.

Factor in a varied landscape of harsh desert, rocky mountains, surf-ready beaches, idyllic vineyards, and densely populated (but rapidly changing) border cities, and learn that to travel, eat, and understand Baja is to love Baja.

ADAM GOLDBERG, EDITOR IN CHIEF

BAJA

● MEXICO CITY

TABLE OF CONTENTS

BAJA, MEXICO

ENRIQUE OLVERA

MANTA, CABO SAN LUCAS
22.89784 ° N, 109.86790 ° W

There is no Mexican chef who has garnered as much praise in recent years as Enrique Olvera. When he opened Pujol—now ranked No. 16 on San Pellegrino's influential World's 50 Best Restaurants list—in Mexico City in 2000, he chose not to serve his grandmother's *mole*. He served *mole* all his own, devising a distinctive style of contemporary Mexican cuisine that employed subtle references to traditional, regional Mexican cooking but never veered into on-the-nose territory. Four restaurants later, including his newly-opened Manta in Los Cabos, and Olvera's still more likely to give you a hug than a handshake. Here, he explains why he scaled back on meat on his menus and how he defines Baja cuisine.

WHAT MADE YOU DECIDE TO OPEN A RESTAURANT IN BAJA?
You just have to look around to understand what a beautiful place this is. Los Cabos is one of the most important beaches in Mexico, but the geography, the sea, and all of the products that are available make it special. Not only is there a lot of tourism coming in, but there's high-end tourism. People who come here are well-traveled and willing to spend money. And since huge restaurants like Charlie Trotter's C have opened, and several famous chefs have come to Los Cabos to open restaurants in different hotels, people are paying attention to Cabo as a food destination. For those reasons, I think Los Cabos has made itself one of the most important gastronomic hubs in Mexico.

YOU'VE BEEN KNOWN TO SAY THAT LOS CABOS IS ONE OF YOUR FAVORITE PLACES TO COME AND RELAX, BUT YOU WOULD NEVER WANT TO OPEN A RESTAURANT HERE. WHAT MADE YOU CHANGE YOUR MIND?
I don't know. I still think about it. I think I like it so much that I needed an excuse to come more often. Fortunately Manta's only serving dinner, so I still have time in the mornings to relax. Then I can come in and work in the evenings. Right now I'm coming here once a month. In general, I think the ambiance of the hotels here helps, because if it were too formal—if Manta were a higher-end restaurant—we'd probably have a lot more pressure to perform. But since we're trying to do something more casual, something that is high-quality and seafood-driven but not stuffy, I feel like I can still relax even though I'm here for work.

WHAT'S THE FOOD FOCUS OF MANTA?
We're trying to serve food from Baja California. Whenever I've come to Los Cabos, I've always craved certain foods—seafood mostly, something very

fresh—and most hotel restaurants can't provide that. If you spend the whole day in the pool relaxing, you don't want to eat a huge piece of steak with a thick sauce. You're probably interested in having ceviche or some clams. We're trying to do something that is relevant to the surroundings and makes you feel comfortable. We wanted to cook food that you would want to eat at night. Because when you're on the beach and it's warm, you don't want to eat something too heavy.

DO YOU USE LOCAL INGREDIENTS OR DO YOU BRING THEM IN FROM ELSEWHERE?
Not everything can be 100 percent local. Most of the fish is; the clams are. But, for example, the meat is not from here. There are a couple of really good vegetable purveyors that provide us with speciality products like cucumbers and other vegetables. In Miraflores, there are a lot of farms, so the beets and some legumes come from there. But we're also bringing in things from other parts of the country, because you just can't get everything you need here, all the time.

HOW DO YOU COMPARE A NEW RESTAURANT LIKE THIS TO YOUR OTHER RESTAURANTS?
Manta is probably a little bit of a mix between Maíz de Mar and Cosme. It has my touch, and I think when you come into one of my restaurants, you can see that it's mine. There is a common language among them. Food-wise, it's closer to Maíz de Mar in Playa del Carmen. I think the black room is reminiscent of Pujol, while the large space is reminiscent of Cosme in New York. It's a mix, but there are definitely little things from all of the restaurants here.

HOW DID YOU GET INTO COOKING?
I started cooking, because I've always liked making people happy. My father started traveling a lot when I was in high school, so I was often home alone and

had to cook for myself. Since there were no parents at home, my friends liked coming over to party and have a good time. I started cooking for them; then I got a reputation for being a good cook and it just kept going.

At that time in Mexico, being a chef was not popular. I don't think it was very popular elsewhere in the world either, but when I went to cooking school, I didn't know to want to be like Fernando Olea or any of these great chefs that now everybody knows. When I thought about cooking, I thought about transforming products, making new flavors, and making people happy.

When you're trying to become a great chef, at some point along the way you sort of lose sight of this. But I think, now in my career, I'm at the point where I just want to go back to enjoying cooking and having people over.

DID YOU END UP GOING TO COOKING SCHOOL?
My father wanted me to have a bachelor's degree, so I enrolled in tourism school in Mexico City. I didn't last more than a month there. I simply stopped going. A month later, I told my father, "I don't know if you've noticed but I haven't been going to school. I've been actually going to a restaurant to work." That's when he realized that I was serious about cooking.

He told me, "If you're going to do the cooking thing, you might as well do it well." So I started investigating, and since the Culinary Institute of America was the best school in the world supposedly, I wanted to go there.

HOW LONG AFTER SCHOOL DID YOU MOVE BACK TO MEXICO?
They give you a six-month work permit when you graduate, so I used that until it expired. Then I went back to Mexico. I still like to think I'm a self-taught chef. I didn't work for a long time with any mentorship under a great chef. It took me a longer time to develop my own cooking style and to understand cooking better, but I also think it's good, because now I have my own style, and I wasn't strongly influenced by any particular chef. I started to create my own language for Mexican cooking. I have a good background in French technique that came

from school, but everything that I've learned about Mexican cooking has been on the job.

NOW PEOPLE SAY THAT YOU'RE REINVENTING MEXICAN CUISINE.
I never liked cooking the same thing that my mother cooked. Even when I was cooking at a very young age, I always liked showing my personality or changing one little thing in the recipe to make it my own. I didn't want to be known as the person who makes my mother's sauce; I wanted to be known for making my own.

That has always been part of my personality, and that's part of my restaurants. It's not that we're trying to do a dish that nobody has made before. It's more about doing something that is a reflection of how you think and approach food.

The set of principles we use isn't new. We like to work with local products. We like to utilize the ingredients completely. We don't like to waste products. We don't think that geometry is important in food. We think that something that is natural and honest is more beautiful than something that is staged and over-produced. You can see those things in the way we plate and cut vegetables. I could probably do more designs, but I like the fact of things that are more organic and simple. I think one beautiful thing in a dish is more than enough. You don't need a hundred things.

YOUR MENUS FIVE YEARS AGO USED TO HAVE MUCH MORE MEAT THAN THEY DO NOW. WHY THE CHANGE?
It's in response to two things. First of all, health. I think fine dining is not considered healthy dining and it makes no sense to me. It's supposed to be the best food in the world and yet it's really bad for you. I wanted my customers to come back, not feel like they needed to go for a run and start dieting the next day.

The other reason is that, in Mexico, it's very difficult to get high-quality animal protein. If you're trying to get a spectacular piece of beef, pork, or even chicken or eggs, it's hard. Production is very limited, and since the providers are usually very small, they also are inconsistent. The one thing that we can get that's beautiful all the time is fruits and vegetables. Plus, they're good for you.

So, instead of having a huge piece of steak with a little vegetable, I like a huge plate of vegetables and maybe the steak becomes the sauce.

DO YOU EAT THAT WAY IN YOUR PERSONAL LIFE?

I try, but I'm never successful. I travel too much, and it's really hard for me to be disciplined, because I'm usually on the move and eating in airports or hotels most of the time. But when I'm home, even if I'm in the hotel, I wake up and have smoked salmon and salad, sometimes with egg whites.

DO YOU COOK WHEN YOU'RE AT HOME?

I'm not home that much, but I like cooking when I'm there. I especially like cooking for my kids and my friends. Sometimes, like on Sundays, I have a good friend with a nice grill who always plays the "Oh, come over. Let's go to the market" trick. We always end up cooking on the grill. I really like it, because it doesn't feel like cooking to me. It just feels like socializing. To me, cooking is what happens in a high-volume restaurant setting. It's not that I'm on the line anymore either. But even if I'm not chopping onions all the time, I feel I'm cooking more than when I do it at home, because at a restaurant, there's never a relaxing moment.

WHAT DO YOU THINK OF WHEN YOU THINK OF BAJA CUISINE?

Baja is a very large region with several different climates. In Ensenada, where you have wine country, there are things that naturally grow around wine—olive trees, almonds—and there's European influence. In Los Cabos, I think it's more about the sea, because it's a desert. Most of what you see is driven by what the sea can give you, because the land is not giving you much.

Nopal, Prickly Pear, and Aloe Vera Salad

FOR THE CURED ALOE

150 g (1 cup) aloe vera leaf

200 g (⅔ cup) sugar

500 g (2 cups) water

FOR THE PRESERVED LEMON

500 g (8 small) yellow lemons

1000 g (3 cups) kosher salt

FOR THE SALAD

100 g (½ cup) nopal, sliced into 1cm thick sticks

30 g (¼ cup) red or green tuna cactus (also red or green prickly pear)

10 g (1 tbsp) lime juice

20 g (2 tbsp) cured lemon, julienne

15 g (3 tbsp) Xoconostle cactus, finely diced

10 g (¼ cup) cilantro leaves

12 g (2 tbsp) red onion, julienne

10 g (¼ cup) purslane

40 g (3 tbsp) extra virgin olive oil

15 g (1 tbsp) cured aloe vera leaf

10 g (2 tbsp) pasilla chile powder

Prep time: 5 days
Assembly time: 15 mins
Serves 2

PART I: CURE THE ALOE

1. Clean and peel the aloe vera.

2. Combine sugar and water. Bring to a boil. Reduce heat to low.

3. Add aloe vera and cook in sugar and water syrup for 3 minutes.

4. Let it cool down and set aside.

PART II: CURE THE LEMON

1. Cut lemons into quarters. Squeeze the juice from the lemons into a small bowl and set aside.

2. Put the lemons into a container and cover them completely with salt.

3. Add squeezed juice from the lemons until it fills ¾ of the container.

4. Leave at room temperature for three days. Lemons should continue to release more juice. Add more lemon juice if lemons appear dry.

5. Let sit at room temperature for three days. After three days are up, put lemons in the fridge and allow to sit for five more days.

PART III: PREPARE THE SALAD

1. Flash cure the nopal by burying it under kosher salt in a bowl. Make sure nopal is completely covered. Let sit for 3 minutes. Then, remove nopal and rinse with water. Set aside and drain.

2. In a serving bowl, dress the tuna cactus (prickly pear) with the lime juice, the cured lemon, and Xoconostle.

3. Place the nopales—still separate—with the rest of the vegetables, and add olive oil.

4. Top with herbs, aloe slices, and red onion. Sprinkle with pasilla chile powder to taste.

IDELFONSO "PONCHO" AVILÉS

BLUE FISH, SAN JOSÉ DEL CABO
23.03834 ° N, 109.70924 ° W

Idelfonso "Poncho" Avilés Agúndez, chef and part-owner at the upmarket fusion restaurant Blue Fish, has witnessed a lot of change in Los Cabos. He was born and raised there, in La Playita, before multimillion-dollar resort and luxury home development deals transformed the place. These days, he mans the kind of restaurant that, despite the price point, breeds devoted regulars among locals and tourists alike. Because when they're at the restaurant, it's not really about them: It's about raw fish, and the seemingly infinite creative combinations Avilés Agúndez can dream up.

WHAT WAS SAN JOSÉ DEL CABO LIKE WHEN YOU WERE GROWING UP?
It was very small and quiet. There was only one paved road that would lead to the entrance of the church. Everything else was dirt roads. One of those roads would take you to what we now refer to as San Vicente, La Choya, and La Playita, where I grew up. There was only one big market, *Goncanseco*.

HOW HAS IT CHANGED SINCE THEN?
I lived here when there were only 8,000 inhabitants. There wasn't much construction back then either; just a one-lane road that would connect San José to Cabo San Lucas and the airport—an old *palapa* where you could sit and wait for the one and only flight that flew here during the daytime because there were no lights. Can you imagine that?

HOW DID YOU GET INTO COOKING?
I used to deliver oysters to a few of the restaurants in town. My family worked with the big boy oysters you could find at La Playita. After school, my uncles would clean the oysters and take them out of the shells. Then they'd give them to me in a big pot, and I'd go around selling them to restaurants or individual houses.

DID YOU CATCH OYSTERS TOO?
Yes. We would go diving; and because oysters are attached to big rocks, we would use a kind of lever to hit and separate the shells from the rocks.

WOULD YOU EVER COOK THEM?
We tend to have them raw, served fresh with lime and chile. But never salt, because they're already salty from the water.

DO YOU STILL EAT FISH WITH YOUR FAMILY?
Not as much, because I work with fish all week.

At home, I make my kids beans, *enfrijoladas*, and *rellenas* with chicken. But their favorite thing is this tuna dip I make. I sneak in vegetables and chipotles. They just sit there and eat it while watching TV.

HOW CAN YOU TELL IF FISH IS FRESH?
You can tell because of the consistency it has when you touch it. It has to be very firm. You can also tell by looking at the fish's eyes. The eyes have to be very shiny. If they're opaque, the fish isn't fresh. The gills should also be a vibrant red color.

DID YOU GET INTO COOKING BECAUSE OF THE FAMILY OYSTER BUSINESS?
Yes, I actually started working at the restaurants where I used to deliver oysters to. Later on, I worked at restaurants serving ceviche and seafood—basically what I serve at Blue Fish, but much more traditional. I would make enough money just to pay the rent and keep on going. When they raised my rent, I had to move out. That's actually how I got set up with my current partners.

BLUE FISH DOESN'T SERVE TRADITIONAL MEXICAN PREPARATIONS OF FISH. WHAT ARE THE INFLUENCES?
Even though my fish a little thicker than the traditional style, I learned Japanese sashimi-style fish cuts from a Japanese chef at the One&Only Palmilla.

For the *ceviche*, the flavors are very different, more Peruvian. Traditional Mexican ceviche has tomato, chile, onion, cilantro, and lime. But I didn't want to offer just that; I wanted to try something I had never tasted before.

HOW DOES THAT TRANSLATE TO THE MENU?
My favorite thing is the mango *ceviche*. I love the way the chile and lemon, along with the sweetness of

the mango, complements the flavor of the fish. Then you get this last kick of ginger. We actually couldn't get Mexican mangos, like the ones I would get at the market, for a long time after Hurricane Odile. We had to bring them in from Ecuador and Peru.

I also experiment with a Mazatlán-style *ceviche* with cucumbers and carrots, another that has pequin pepper and *jícama*, and a version with olives and cilantro. But I usually have to use different fish—cabrilla instead of sierra—than I normally would, because many Americans think that some fish smell and taste too "fishy."

DO YOU SEE A DIFFERENCE IN WHAT LOCALS AND TOURISTS ORDER?
Locals order everything raw—*ceviches, aguachiles.* Most tourists come asking for cooked foods. Even if it's the most perfect fish, they're always saying, "It smells" or something. But you can't get fresher fish than what we have here. They don't trust raw fish much, and they're also always asking for tacos. But I am actually most scared of the older women who come in. They know their fish well, and aren't afraid to tell you what they think, so everything has to be perfect.

White Fish Ceviche with Mango

150 g (1 cup) white fish, such as sea bass, pacific halibut, cod, or grouper

45 g (3 tbsp) fresh lime juice (Mexican limes, if available)

30 g (2 tbsp) fresh orange juice

120 g (¾ cup) ripe mango

4 g (½ tsp) finely chopped red onion

2 g (½ tsp) finely chopped fresh serrano peppers

2 g (½ tsp) finely chopped ginger

10 g (2 tsp) extra virgin olive oil

1 g (½ tsp) cilantro

1 g (½ tsp) piquin (pequin) pepper powder

6 g (1 tsp) sea salt

Prep time: 15 minutes
Assembly time: 5 minutes
Serves 2

1. Chop fish into small 1 cm cubes and place in a small bowl. Add half of the lime juice. Let the combined white fish and lime sit for 5 minutes.

2. Add the fresh orange juice and remainder of lime juice.

3. Chop the ripe mango into small 1 cm cubes and place in a second medium-sized bowl.

4. Add red onion, serrano peppers, ginger, and olive oil to the ripe mango.

5. Gently combine the mango mixture using a wooden spoon.

6. Lastly, add cilantro, piquin pepper powder, and a pinch of salt to the medium-sized bowl.

7. Add the cubed white fish from the small bowl, and gently combine all ingredients.

8. Serve in a cold ceviche container or wide serving bowl.

Shrimp Tacos in Jicama Tortillas

10 g (2 tsp) extra virgin olive oil

6 g (1 tsp) table salt

5 g (1 clove) garlic

120 g (approx. 6) uncooked jumbo shrimp, peeled and deveined

15 g (2 tbsp) red cabbage, finely sliced into strips

15 g (2 tbsp) white cabbage, finely sliced into strips

10 g (¼ pepper) fresh habanero pepper, thinly sliced

2 slices (2 mm thick) peeled jicama, thinly sliced lengthwise, in the shape of a "tortilla"

30 g (2 tbsp) fresh lime juice (Mexican limes, if available)

Prep time: 10 minutes
Cooking time: 10 minutes
Serves 2

1. Add half of the olive oil and half of the finely chopped garlic to a cast iron skillet over medium-high heat. Add shrimp to sear. Turn over shrimp in 3 to 5 minutes, or once they begin to brown. Add a pinch of salt to taste.

2. In a separate small pan, add remaining olive oil, chopped garlic, and the red and white cabbage, along with the habanero pepper. Stir until cabbage becomes translucent, 3 to 5 minutes. Add a pinch of salt to taste.

3. Place the two tortilla-thin slices of jicama on a serving plate.

4. Add sauteed cabbage to each slice of jicama, and place 3 shrimp on each.

5. Add more cabbage to each taco, and drizzle with lime juice to taste.

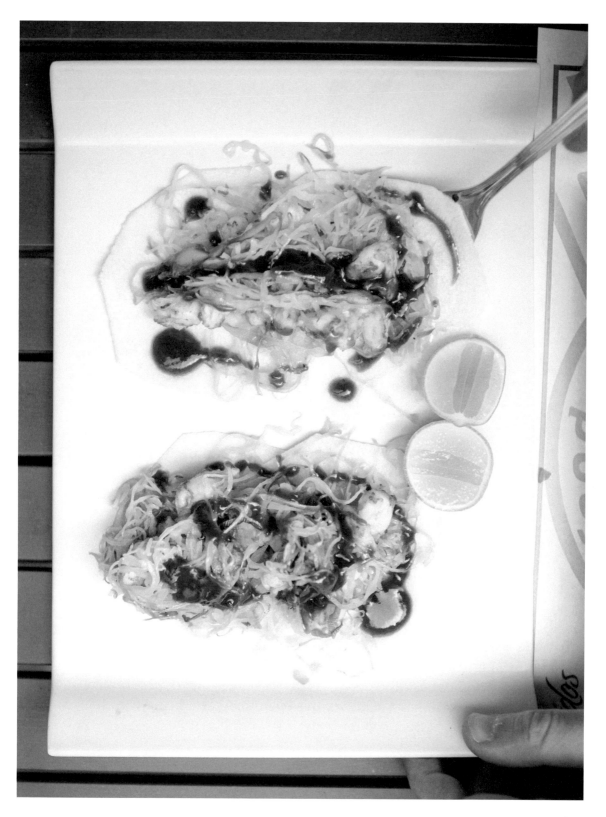

CARLOS VALDEZ

BUFFALO BBQ, LA PAZ
24.14695 ° N, 110.3380 ° W

Chef Carlos Valdez spends most of his time around flames. At his restaurant Buffalo BBQ in La Paz, Valdez commands a wood-burning grill, wielding a mix of styles spanning from his home state of Sonora to the U.S., Japan, and Argentina. To hear him speak of fire, and the grill it powers, is to witness deep reverence and intuition. It's no wonder then that his restaurant is one of the most exciting in Baja, both for its charismatic and talented chef, and the wide array of soul-gratifying shellfish and meat consumed there.

WHEN DID YOU FIRST START COOKING?
I started cooking as a kid with my mom, who is an excellent cook, and I always liked it. For example, when I turned 15, it's a Mexican tradition to have a party with lots of beer. My uncle, who was the Secretary of Fisheries in those days in Sonora, asked what I wanted for my birthday. I said I wanted a loggerhead turtle, *caguama*—it was legal at the time, of course. But I told him, "I want you to take me to the master of the loggerhead and tell him to teach me how to cook it." He took me to the famous Pancho, *El Caguamero*. And I spent my fifteenth birthday cooking a loggerhead with him. That was my first real cooking lesson, and it was the first thing I learned to do well.

HAD YOU COOKED BEFORE THEN?
I knew how to grill and all that. But that day with *El Caguamero* was really how it all began. I started cooking, and cooking, and cooking.

HOW DID YOU KNOW THAT'S WHAT YOU WANTED TO DO?
I didn't. I was really good at math, so when it was time to go to college, and my dad asked me what I was going to study, he was not happy when I told him I wanted to study gastronomy. At that time, around the late '70s and early '80s, gastronomy as a career had a bad reputation. Meanwhile, now it's a hip thing to go to college for—probably the most expensive, too. He told me that because I was good at math, I would be studying engineering. No discussion. I liked engineering enough. When I graduated, I went to Ciudad Obregón. My dad was proud and figured I'd work as a civil engineer. What do you think I did?

WORKED AS A COOK?
No, not yet. Despite being a civil engineer, up until

that point, the only thing I had built in my whole life was a *palapa*. So, I built a *palapa* on a piece of land, and started to cook lobster and fish and make cocktails. It became my very own small restaurant.

WHAT WAS THE NAME OF THE PLACE?
The first one was called Nikos. It was about cheese, wine, and the sea.

HOW DID YOU END UP IN LA PAZ?
Sonora has a lot of shrimp and crab, but I really wanted to cook lobster, abalone, and sea urchin. I started traveling to Baja for it. I bought a refrigerated truck, and I basically put a fish market next to my restaurant. Years later, I came back to La Paz and got married here.

WHAT WAS IT LIKE WHEN YOU OPENED YOUR FIRST BAJA RESTAURANT?
Right now, we are doing very well, thankfully. But it was very difficult to establish anything here. Before I got here, everything was deep fried and all about fish tacos. The wines were served hot. There was no culture of good service. When we arrived 12 years ago, we started by roasting meat, doing *carne asada*. Obviously my cooking style has evolved since then. I now say my kitchen cooks the cuisine of the Sea of Cortez.

We also serve more interesting tacos these days: for instance, a *taco paceño* with *chicharrón* of ribeye, lobster and grasshoppers in a beet tortilla, with red chile.

WHAT IS BAJA FOOD TO YOU?
It is very different from what's in Baja Norte, where there was a lot of Chinese and Mediterranean influence. That part of Baja has a sort of Mediterranean climate, so that's really defined their

cuisine. I'd say we're more rustic here. It's historically been an isolated area where everything came in by boat. A cooking style developed among the fisherman—sausage made of grouper cheeks, *flautas* made of whatever they caught that day—and an interesting cuisine developed.

WHAT DO YOU MEAN?
For instance, many fishing communities were isolated and there was no ice, so fisherman would dry fish to preserve it. There were lots of interesting little things like that. We have here a few valleys, like in San Juan de la Costa, where orange trees—the original Valencia orange—were planted by Spanish missionaries. You can no longer find it in Spain, and yet they are here. The islands here are full of goats. Isn't it kind of crazy that I ask fishermen for goats?

Then I think about the 80 percent of people here who are from Sinaloa or Sonora, and how they brought with them ways of cultivating cattle. The best *machaca* is here in La Paz—not in Sonora, but here. They dry it, roast it, and add wild oregano and garlic when they're grinding it. We also have a lot of chicken here and six or seven months of good local vegetable production.

ARE TORTILLAS HERE USUALLY CORN OR FLOUR?
Flour, for sure. There is corn, but it's not the main thing in Baja, because we've adopted some things from Sonora. I say this because the best tortilla is in Ciudad Obregón in Sonora. They add a bit of cheese—*requesón*—to add a buttery feel to them.

YOU MENTIONED YOU COULD EAT THIS FOOD EVERYDAY. WHY IS THAT?
I began cooking shellfish because I love them so much. In Ciudad Obregón, Sonora, where I'm from, there's a street called Guerrero, where every corner has a seafood cart or restaurant of some kind. The whole street smells like octopus. I'm not kidding. I used to eat there everyday.

We had lemon trees at my house, too, so I would stuff huge bags with lemons and take them to the seafood carts. I would give them the bag for *pata de mula* clams or maybe some oysters. They always laughed because I was a little kid bartering for shellfish, but I loved it.

WHEN YOU EAT SHELLFISH, HOW DO YOU PREPARE IT?
Just with lemon. I like to really taste it.

WHY DO YOU THINK ADDING LEMON IS THE BEST WAY TO TASTE IT?
Popular belief says that if there is a bug or bacteria, lemon kills it. But I really like the acid of the lemon with the sweetness of the clams here. There are other clams—razor clams, chocolate clams—that have more minerals in the flavor, because the largest phosphate mine, called Rofomex, or Mexican rock phosphate, is right on the other side of the bay.

HOW DO YOU PREPARE THE RAZOR CLAMS USUALLY?
I really like to grill them Galician style. I open them up, add some olive oil, parsley, lemon, and garlic, and then put them right on a plate.

WHEN YOU COOK OCTOPUS, HOW DO YOU MAKE THE SKIN CRUNCHY AND THE INSIDE SOFT?
The grill gives the crispiness to the skin. I always add a little oil and wine to get the flame going. That's what gives the outside its crunch. I learned how to get the soft inside when I was in Japan. They told me to add wakame, and nothing else. It works. Now I always try to add a Japanese touch to my cooking.

WHY WERE YOU IN JAPAN?
I cook in Japan every year, as a guest of the Mexican Embassy in Tokyo. Since we export abalone, lobster, and other shellfish from here to Japan, I get invited to go and cook once a year.

YOU'RE OPENING ANOTHER RESTAURANT SOON. WILL THAT BE YOUR FIRST RESTAURANT OUTSIDE OF LA PAZ?
Yes. I chose Los Cabos because it's nearby, so I can attend to both. I'm working with European partners, and it's an ambitious project. It's on seven hectares with a canyon that has more than 500 palm trees and a stream of fresh water. It's right next to the Thompson Hotel there. We'll start with Buffalo BBQ and an area for events. The second phase will be building a boutique hotel with 40 rooms and enough space to build houses. What sells for 1,000 pesos here per month will sell for 6,000 in Cabo. Here in La Paz, things are happening. But Cabo is really booming.

WHY IS YOUR RESTAURANT CALLED BUFFALO BBQ?
I was in the northern states of the U.S. 12 years ago, and I tried buffalo meat. I just loved it, and said, "I'm taking buffalo to Mexico." I tried ribs and buffalo burgers. So I started selling buffalo meat and named the restaurant Buffalo. But then we weren't able to get meat from the U.S. or Canada because of mad cow disease.

YOU MOSTLY USE A BLENDER AND A GRILL AT THE RESTAURANT. WHY?
I feel like buying other stuff would lose some of the magic. I really love grilling—the fire, the smoke, and all of those things that come with it. I never use a thermometer, ever. When you spend so much time with fire, there is really a communication between you and the grill. It becomes pure intuition at some point.

WHAT IS IT ABOUT THE GRILL THAT DRAWS YOU IN?
Fire was the first expression of heat experienced by humans. It's mystical to a certain extent—magical. When you love fire, there is a weird communication. You understand fire: how hot it is, and how it becomes different when the evening arrives. Every meat has its own cooking time, too. A rib-eye from Sonora cooks differently than a rib-eye from Nebraska.

BECAUSE OF FAT?
Yes, exactly. That's the thing. I understand fire. I've been grilling for 20 years; sleeping and dreaming of roasting food over a fire.

HAS YOUR STYLE OF GRILLING CHANGED OVER THE PAST 20 YEARS?
The oil I use for the fish and the meat, and the herb sauce I use as a spread for meat, are all the same. I think the technique is the same, too. But what's changed is my perspective. I started grilling in Sonora. But I began to study, travel, and see how it was done elsewhere. I saw how Americans did it or how the Argentines grilled. So my style is a fusion of everything—what I've seen in Cleveland or Argentina or Sonora, Texas, Arizona. I've become faster and more experience on the grill, too, of course.

IS THERE A RIGHT WAY TO GRILL?
Yes. For example, Sinaloan grilling is really Argentine. You go to a restaurant and they have all the meat on the grill, even if not requested. We are very similar to Arizona or Texas here. The places in Mexico that really know how to roast are Sonora, Chihuahua, Nuevo León, and Baja right now. That's pretty much it. The rest is different.

ANY GRILLING TIPS FOR HOME COOKS?
One thing very few people take into account is that, before grilling the meat, it should sit out for two hours. That helps the fat begin to flow, and the meat becomes more naturally lubricated. Many people— many professional cooks, too—take the meat directly from the refrigerator and place it right onto the fire. That creates stress; there's a sudden change in temperature, since the cold meat is going right onto hot heat. Europeans, or the Spanish, have the meat outside throughout the service and slice it at the moment you ask for it. If it's warm, it doesn't matter. That makes it tender.

Another important thing to remember is salt. On good meat, put good salt and nothing else. Maybe put a little olive oil to lubricate it, but that's really it.

WHAT ABOUT COOKING FISH OR OCTOPUS?
Fish should definitely be cold before grilling. Fish does not hold heat in the same way. I love placing it in olive oil, though. What I do is completely cover the fish in olive oil so there is no contact with the atmosphere, and therefore, no oxidation. Fatty fish oxidize very quickly. Then I take it right out of the olive oil and put it on the fire.

HOW DO YOU COME UP WITH YOUR RECIPES?
I'm self-taught, and I'm really happy I didn't study cooking, actually. I am passionate about books, so whenever I'm in the U.S. or around Mexico, I buy cookbooks or food magazines. I look at so many, and ideas start brewing. I spend a huge portion of my life reading. I don't watch TV.

For example, I'll go for a walk along the boardwalk, and think and think. By the time I get back, I have two or three new recipe ideas. I'm really in my own world.

White Clam with Seaweed Aguachile

15 g (½ cup) dried wakame

40 g (2 ¾ tbsp) wate

100 g (2 cups chopped) spinach

100 g (2 cups chopped) cilantro

250 g (1 cup chopped) sea lettuce (ulva lactuca)

50 g serrano pepper

200 g (¾ cup) fresh lime juice

6 live white clams

0.5 g (1 pinch) sea salt

Prep time: 12 hours
Assembly time: 15 minutes
Serves 2

1. Place wakame in water for 20 to 30 minutes to rehydrate.

2. Add wakame and water mixture with remaining ingredients into a blender and blend on high until smooth. Save a few pieces of sea lettuce for garnish.

3. Place mixture into a sealed container and let sit in refrigerator overnight.

4. Pass the mixture through a filter bag or fine sieve to remove roughage. Collect the chlorophyll aguachile that passes through.

5. Loosen the clam from its shell and remove its stomach to clean. Put clam back on its shell.

6. Place some ice in a bowl and lay a few pieces of remaining sea lettuce across the top. Use this as a serving plate for the clams.

7. Place the clams on the sea lettuce bed. Before serving, add chlorophyll aguachile to each shell. Optional: Add a pinch of salt to taste.

8. Eat with your hands, or use small fork.

"Mosaic" of Snail and Fresh Vegetables

FOR THE SNAILS

1 kg (approx. 250 g of snail meat) snails, preferably caracoles burros (donkey snails)

1.5 kg (6 ¼ cups) water

30 g (5 ¼ tsp) sea salt

15 g (3 ½ tbsp) japanese mustard

30 g (2 tbsp) tequila

FOR THE SAUCE

250 g (1 cup) snail juice (liquid remaining in pressure cooker), cooled

120 g (½ cup) clamato

70 g (3 ½ tbsp) salsa negra (can be substituted with any dark, smoky salsa)

70 g (4 ¾ tbsp) fresh lime juice

0.5 g (1 pinch) sea salt to taste

0.5 (1 pinch) black pepper to taste

FOR THE "MOSAIC"

12 g (1 tbsp) sesame oil

12 g (1 tbsp) extra virgin olive oil

500 g cooked snail

80 g (10-15 medium-sized) cherry tomatoes

50 g (5 tbsp) diced red onion

10 slices of fresh jalapeño, seeds removed

10 slices of radish

15 g chopped ginger

40 g cucumber, sliced length-wise and rolled

25 g (1 ¾ tbsp) fresh lime juice

0.5 g (1 pinch) sea salt to taste

1. Place snail in pressure cooker on low heat along with water, sea salt, mustard, and tequila. Once the cooker starts whistling, set a timer for 27 minutes.

2. Release pressure from the cooker, taking care not to open until all pressure is removed. Snails should remain in their own juice.

3. Mix sauce. Keep refrigerated.

4. In a large dish with curved edges, add sesame and olive oil to the bottom of the plate. Place cooked snail on top.

5. Garnish dish with cherry tomato, jalapeño, radish, chopped ginger, and rolled cucumber.

6. Season with sea salt and a splash of lime juice.

Prep time: 1 hour
Assembly time: 15 minutes
Serves 4

JUSTINO "EL PROFE" ARCE

ALMEJAS TATEMADAS (BY REQUEST), LORETO
26.00944 ° N, 111.33926 ° W

They call him "El Profe"—the professor.

Born in Loreto, Justino Arce Fernández knows his clams. For decades, he has been working with *almejas chocolatas*, or chocolate clams, a beautiful bivalve with a brown shell abundant in the warm waters of El Mar de Cortés in Baja Sur. He and his family were the first to grade clams in the area, and now he's best known as the purveyor of Loreto's sublime *almejas tatemadas*: chocolate clams strewn over an open fire, grilled and slightly charred to perfection. Eat them on the beach and soak in Loreto's deep seaside quiet—it's what El Profe loves most.

WHAT IS A CHOCOLATE CLAM?
A chocolate clam is a mollusk that thrives on a 30 km stretch of Loreto's coastline. We mainly work here in the small ports in and around Loreto, where it's most abundant.

HOW DO YOU GET THE CLAMS?
Chocolate clam extraction has traditionally been done by free-diving with just our lungs, snorkels, and fins. As time passed, extraction became legalized and there were authorization permits given out, which turned the area into a marine park and gave us the opportunity to use oxygen tanks. Chocolate clams reproduce more or less every four years.

EVERY FOUR YEARS?
In year one, the clam begins to reproduce, even though it's very small. After four years, it grows a lot, so the size is appropriate for extraction and trade. The most important thing is that it starts reproducing from year one, so it releases eggs every season. That's one of the great advantages of the chocolate clam.

Chocolate clams mainly live in warmer waters. Traditionally, many people think that clams deposit the eggs right where they are buried, but that's not the case. Roe rises, and then when it's ripe, it falls. So there are times when you find yourself in places where you do not think there can be possibly be any clams, but they're there. The currents actually carry the roe long distances, and then it falls in places favorable for development.

WHEN DID YOU FIRST GET INVOLVED WITH CLAMS?
Right now, I'm 50 years old, but I started when I was 11 with my dad. I've spent all my life working with chocolate clams. We grade chocolate clams for Loreto. When there are visitors to the area—a president or some other important person—we prepare clams and talk about them. There are several people who do this, but my family and I founded the practice.

WHAT DISTINGUISHES THE CHOCOLATE CLAM?
It's about its taste, color, and smell. If you bring me a clam, I can tell you whether it's from Bahía Concepción or Juncalito; Ensenada Blanca or here in Loreto. For example, when you cook Bahia Concepción's clams, the juice is light brown, and the clams in Loreto don't have that. Their juice is white. Then there are clams in San Carlos that are a little bigger than the ones from Loreto.

IS THERE A BAN ON FISHING THEM RIGHT NOW?
What's happening now is that there are permits with built-in quotas. Usually, the quota is the number of kilos of clams you can extract over a certain period of time. So, if you max out the quota in two or days, that's your problem.

IS THIS A WAY TO PROTECT THE CLAMS?
In a way, yes. But I think there are people who are not native to Loreto—people from other states—that want to monopolize the trade. What we say is: "Small town, big hell."

WHAT IS THE MOST TRADITIONAL WAY OF EATING OR COOKING THE CLAMS?
The traditional way of preparing and eating clams is *tatemada*, or charred. You can also eat them in their shells or pickled in cream. The pickled clams have to be cooked first and left in salted water for three to four hours. Once they're cooked, take them out, clean them, and remove the shell. Dunk them in a pressure cooker for about 40 to 45 minutes to soften them.

Then serve with mustard, oil, and vinegar. But it's the *tatemada* that really represents Loreto.

WHAT'S THE BEST WAY TO PREPARE ALMEJAS TATEMADAS?
One of the interesting things about *almejas tatemadas* is that you have to use 100 percent live, caught-that-day clams. In cold weather, clams can last two days. But during summertime or in the very hot weather, they only last a day or, sometimes, only half a day, depending on the heat.

HOW DO YOU KNOW IF THEY ARE ALIVE?
When they are dead, they splay open; when alive, they're shut tight. The color also changes each day. First they're dark brown; the second day, they're a little lighter.

HOW DO THEY KEEP BEST THEN?
You can teach yourself how to care for them. It mostly consists of putting them in salt water, away from the sun.

STEP ONE IS MAKING SURE THE CLAMS ARE ALIVE AND FRESH. WHAT'S STEP TWO FOR COOKING THEM TATEMADAS?
It all takes place on a bed of gravel, which is really just small pebbles from the beach. You place the clams face down, with the opening downwards, very close together. The approximate number of clams per person is about 12. Multiply that by how many people you're cooking for. When you have them all placed face-down, you add more gravel on top to cover them.

From there, add wood. We use *romerillo*, a type of weed that can be found near the beach, especially near streams. You place it on top and light fire to it. When it's lit, you spread the ashes and let that sit for 45 minutes. After 45 minutes, you can test the clams, preferably one from the center because those would be the least cooked, and then try one from the edges.

IF WE DON'T HAVE ROMERILLO, WHAT COULD WE USE?
Any type of tumbleweed or thin branch works. It'll smell great, and give the clams a nice smoky flavor.

HOW DO YOU KNOW WHEN THE ONE IN THE CENTER IS ALREADY COOKED?
Because it opens. If it's not open, it means that the clam is still raw. It should open easily once you try to open it.

WHAT HAPPENS ONCE THEY'RE READY?
Once they're cooked, grab the clams and open them. You can make tacos with flour tortillas. They're usually topped with mustard dressing, which is a mix of jalapeño pepper, mustard, oil, and vinegar. Everyone has their magic recipe for that acidic sauce. All that's left after the sauce is to make the taco with the clams and the dressing. Then, eat.

DO YOU EAT CLAMS AT HOME, TOO?
We actually eat very few clams. Since we work with them all day, we don't really crave them. But when my daughters are home—one works in La Paz—we go snorkeling for clams. They can take 100 to 200 clams between the two of them. It's good exercise for me; it helps keep me fit.

WHAT WAS LORETO LIKE WHEN YOU FIRST STARTED DOING THIS?
Traditionally, *almejas tatemadas* was a dish that was consumed at the edge of the beach. There used to be large trees all along the shore, and on Saturdays and Sundays, families would spend all day at the beach. They would get their clams and make them *tatemadas*. Usually each family had its own spot to get its clams. As time passed, Loreto grew: There were city-wide projects in the works, and people were moving here from elsewhere. The population grew and that tradition sort of got lost.

WHY?
I think it had a lot to do with construction on the beach that removed the trees. Then there were those who dared to commercialize that tradition.

WHAT DO FOREIGNERS THINK OF ALMEJAS TATEMADAS?
Some don't like them, but the vast majority do. What attracts attention to them is that the process is 100 percent natural—no preservatives, no chemicals, nothing like that. That seems to be mainly what people from other countries seek. I think it's one of the healthiest products we have. Chicken is injected, cattle is injected, but it's very difficult for people to add chemicals to these to make them grow faster. The only thing that we should try to do is keep our beaches clean.

WAS LORETO ALWAY'S A DESTINATION FOR TOURISTS?
Loreto was a small village dedicated to fishing and tourism mainly. There were people, mostly Americans, bringing people by plane for fishing. Loreto really isn't ready for mass tourism.

WHY?
There aren't enough hotels, and it requires a lot of investment to make that happen. We'd prefer tourism to stay how it is right now: peaceful and relaxed. The Americans that visit us here are mostly elderly. Young people who travel for nightlife can't really find that here, because Loreto doesn't really have that. Perhaps the real attraction here is tranquility.

Loreto-Style Charred Clams (Almejas Tatemadas)

24 live chocolate clams (can substitute with large clams)

10 branches or large twigs, preferably romerillo

1/2 bucket gravel

120 g (1/2 cup) yellow mustard

30 g (2 tbsp) extra virgin olive oil

2 jalapeño peppers

26 g (2 tbsp) white vinegar

Prep time: 2 hours
Cooking time: 1 hour
Serves 4

1. Make sure clams are alive and fresh.

2. Create a bed of gravel and place the open clams face down, with the hinge of the shell facing up. Clams will be vertical, not horizontal. Pack close together.

3. Cover with a layer of gravel.

4. Place romerillo on top of the gravel and light fire to it.

5. When the wood is consumed, spread ashes over the top and let sit for 45 minutes.

6. While cooking, make the mustard dressing. Mix mustard, jalapeño pepper, olive oil, and vinegar in a blender until liquefied. Place mix in a sauce bowl.

6. After 45 minutes, check a clam or two—preferably one from the center and one from the edge—to see whether they are open and cooked through.

7. Once cooked, open clams and top with mustard dressing. They can also be enjoyed taco-style in flour tortillas.

ELVA ESPINOZA
MAMA ESPINOZA, EL ROSARIO
27.68607 ° N, 113.41166 ° W

Four hours north of Santa Rosalía and four hours south of Ensenada, roadtrippers find themselves driving through a long expanse of desert with little hope of finding a rest stop. At least that used to be the case, before Ana Grosso Peña, also known as "Mama Espinoza" and born in 1906, opened a restaurant of the same name and wooed hungry Baja 1000 racecar drivers with her lobster burritos. Everybody in Baja knows Mama Espinoza, a 109-year-old living legend, and now her daughter, Elva Espinoza, runs the restaurant. In the years since Elva's taken over, she's been charged with one task: not changing a thing.

WHAT WAS MAMA ESPINOZA LIKE WHEN IT FIRST OPENED?
Fifty years ago, the restaurant was only a few feet wide with only a wood-burning stove. It wasn't until 35 years ago that we expanded to multiple rooms. Now we have the luxury of stainless steel equipment and furniture, instead of just a small wooden table. We still try to keep everything as clean as possible, because this is Mama Espinoza's actual house.

SHE STILL LIVES HERE?
Yes, this is her real home. She is turning 109 years old this year. She had 16 children in this house. I'm the seventh one—her only daughter now—and I'm the one who continues to manage the business.

HOW DID MAMA ESPINOZA START?
My mother got married in 1930 to my father, a rancher. She was a lucky girl. Her father was Italian, from Genoa, and his family moved to Santa Rosalía for the El Boleo Mine. At that time, many French, Italians, Norwegians—people of all nationalities, and many young people from Europe—came to work at El Boleo Mine. My grandfather fell in love with a housekeeper, got her pregnant, and left to go back to Italy. But he returned. Love breaks down barriers.

Years later, my grandfather—my father's father—knew his son wouldn't be rich, so he gifted him and my mom a small house. My grandmother taught him English. And my mom, Mama Espinoza, started selling bean burritos and lobster burritos in flour tortillas. That's how it all began.

WHAT WAS IT LIKE IN 1930?
El Rosario was a village with few families: Peralta, Murillo, Duarte, Espinoza, Garcia, and Valladolid. At that time, they were all *compadres*, or just very good friends. They would bring things for each other:

"*Compadre*, I'll exchange this lobster for a kilo of rice or sugar." There was a need for money, but there was not a love of money.

WAS MAMA ESPINOZA ALWAYS THE NAME?
No, it used to be Casa Espinoza. But then the Baja 1000 [an off-road car race that takes place on Mexico's Baja California Peninsula every November] started in the 1960s. And with that, the restaurant took off. Drivers like Parnelli Jones would call her Mama Espinoza when they would stop here, and they'd tell their friends they ate lobster burritos at Mama Espinoza's.

DO THE RIDERS FROM BAJA 1000 STILL STOP HERE?
Yes. And she still asks, "Where are my friends? You know, the Americans, the founders of the Baja 1000?"

HOW DID YOU END UP IN CHARGE OF THE RESTAURANT?
My mom got offers from others who wanted to buy the property—mostly from people from Tijuana, people that had another vision—but my mother wanted her children to take over. I was married and living in Ensenada. I had five children in school, but once I heard my mother was going to sell the place, I knew I wanted to work here. Because I had a son studying engineering, another one studying law, and my daughters in school, too, we really had no money. But we came anyway, and now we've been here for 26 years already. And we're thankful we still have my mom here with us.

DID SHE INVENT ALL THE RECIPES?
The famous lobster one, absolutely. My mom told me I could never change it.

WHAT DOES IT ENTAIL?
She parboils the lobster, and then takes all the meat

out. She squeezes the meat out of the legs, the claws, and the tail until all of the meat is taken out of the lobster. She never added anything to that—just boiled and placed it in a tortilla, rolled it up, and placed it on the grill. Those were the lobster burritos. The *ranchera* lobster is the tastiest of all because it is raw lobster seasoned with chile, tomato, and onion.

We always serve our burritos in flour tortillas. If you see a dish with a corn tortilla from this area, it's probably a newer chef and the recipe is probably from 2015. But the recipe from the 1930s that my mother goes by always uses flour tortillas.

WHERE DOES THE LOBSTER FOR THE BURRITOS COME FROM?
The lobster we use here comes from the cooperative, named Cooperativa Ensenada. At one point in time, a group of fishermen formed a partnership with a cooperative that sells me the lobster. Before, we could buy it from one of the fishermen here on the beach. It was very cheap to go out and buy it myself. But now everything is sold through the cooperative.

It's still very fresh. We are very privileged here in El Rosario, because our beach abuts the Pacific, which is where the best lobster comes from. Caribbean lobster has a completely different flavor. Since lobster is sometimes very expensive, we also try to make the same recipe with crab.

We now make crab omelets, crab cakes, and crab hamburgers. Though the best is our crab soup.

WHAT DO YOU USE TO COOK IT?
I only use olive oil, salt, pepper, and sometimes butter. We also love making octopus *ranchero*.

WHAT'S THAT?
You parboil octopus. If octopus is very soft, it is not good. Octopus needs texture to make it taste good. With that in mind, when it is at the right point, we slice the tentacles and add prepared *ranchera* sauce. You let it all simmer for a while with the sauce, then serve it with some shrimp soup.

ARE THE LOBSTER BURRITOS THE MAIN DRAW?
Most people don't stop because of the food actually. It is *the* go-to pitstop, at the perfect location for people to rest, get a cup of coffee, a glass of water. You know

you can relax here and find a bathroom. When you make the same drive later on, you remember that the place is very welcoming, and you come back.

Not everyone who comes eats the lobster burrito either. I think maybe 20 out of 100 people eat the lobster burritos. We call it an "obligation stop" because people's bodies need rest, because they need water, and because they need to hear someone else speak after driving in the desert for hours.

The best part for us is that people stopping by feel like they're at home. As my mom always says, "My house is your house."

_____

Crab Soup

250 g *(1 ½ cups) crab meat*

170 g *(1 medium-sized) tomato*

200 g *(1 medium-sized) sweet onion, such as Vidalia*

120 g *(1 medium) whole fresh California or pasilla chile*

750 g *(3 ¼ cups) shrimp broth. If you do not have shrimp broth, you can substitute with a 50/50 mix of seafood stock and water*

15 g *(1 tbsp) extra virgin olive oil*

1 *lime wedge*

Prep time: 15 minutes
Cooking time: 10 minutes
Serves 4

1. Remove crab from shell, and place into a medium-sized bowl.

2. Dice the tomato, onion, and chile.

3. Use a tbsp of olive oil to cook the vegetables for 1 to 2 minutes in a pan. Add crab meat to pan and stir gently until cooked—that is, when color appears reddish—about 4 minutes.

4. Add the vegetable and crab meat mixture to a bowl with warmed shrimp broth. If not yet warm, heat on stove on low heat for until simmering. Garnish with lime wedge.

57

Crab Chile Relleno

FOR THE SAUCE

340 g   (2 medium-sized) tomatoes

100 g   (½ medium-sized) sweet onion

120 g   (1 medium) whole fresh California
or pasilla chile

15 g   (1 tbsp) extra virgin olive oil

0.5 g   (1 pinch) of salt

120 g   (½ cup) chicken broth

FOR THE CHILE

240 g   (2 medium) whole fresh California
or pasilla chiles

250 g   fresh crab meat

200 g   (1 medium-sized) sweet onion

80 g   (2 sticks) celery

5 g   (1 tsp) extra virgin olive oil

Prep time: 25 minutes
Assembly time: 5 minutes
Serves 2

1. First, prepare the sauce by putting the tomatoes, onion, chile, olive oil, salt, and chicken broth in a pot over medium-high heat. Once it begins to bubble, reduce heat and let simmer for 7 to 8 minutes, until all ingredients soften. Set aside.

2. Char the chiles over a grill or gas stove, turning until outside begins to blacken. When they're almost completely blackened and charred, put them in a sealed plastic bag and let sit for 3 to 4 minutes. This allows the chiles to sweat; it makes the skin easier to remove.

3. After 4 minutes, remove the chiles' skin by rinsing under running water.

4. Cut open one side of the chile and remove the seeds.

5. Dice onion and celery.

6. Cook the crab meat with olive oil, onions, and celery for 3 to 4 minutes.

7. Stuff chiles, one at a time, with the crab meat mixture.

8. Place filled peppers on a plate and top generously with sauce.

ALAN PASIANO

MARISCOS EL PIZÓN, ENSENADA
31.83894 ° N, 116.60688 ° W

Do not leave Ensenada without a pitstop at Mariscos El Pizón, a stand where chef Alan Pasiano intermingles avocados and homemade salsa with heaps of fresh sea urchin—*erizo*—atop *tostadas*, as if it's the world's most ordinary and abundant ingredient. Born in Los Cabos, Pasiano is a thoughtful and religious man, who borrowed the name "Pizón" from a river mentioned in the Bible's book of Genesis. A sea urchin expert, he has cleaned and rated them at the famous Tsukiji market in Tokyo and spent years diving for them in Mexico's fertile waters. These days, a trip to his El Pizón culminates the moment your tostada is ready. Eyes wide, you'll wonder: Is all that really for me?

WHERE WERE YOU BORN?
I was born in Los Cabos in March of 1951. My father arrived from Sinaloa and fell in love with my mother, who is from Los Cabos. I also have three daughters.

HOW DID YOU GET TO ENSENADA?
My mother brought me in a tiny boat of about 30 feet. The ship was called *Maria Dolores*. It took like 25 days because the boat was very small and creaky and moved very slowly.

WHAT WAS THAT LIKE?
I remember the ship had a small kitchen that smelled like diesel fuel, banana, and more bananas. I remember that strong smell of food. I can't really see the boat in my memory anymore; I can only smell it.

HOW DID YOU END UP OPENING A SEAFOOD STAND?
It was fate. I very much believe in God. I had nine brothers, and I'm the oldest; I started working as a child. By age 16, I started diving near one of the local islands.

HOW DID YOU GET STARTED DIVING?
I joined a fishing company and started fishing. But my first diving job involved diving for abalone I basically dove for sea urchin and handed them over to the shipowners. I eventually hired some workers and began to export sea urchin to Japan. It was great money.

HOW DO THE JAPANESE PREPARE SEA URCHIN?
They just eat it plain. They might add some wasabi or soy sauce, but it's not necessary. They don't eat it with lime or salt, the way we do here.

DO YOU STILL EXPORT TO JAPAN?
Yes, my sister is actually doing the job I started. I neglected it because I fell into addiction. When one neglects things, someone takes them—and who better than my sister? I could be mad, but I'm not, because no one can be blamed for something I did. Addicts tend to blame someone else, but we are guilty of our own decisions. I was grown and not a child anymore; I was 42 years old.

THERE ARE SO MANY SEAFOOD STANDS HERE IN ENSENADA, BUT NOT MANY HAVE SEA URCHIN. WHY DO YOU FOCUS ON IT?
Exactly. No one else has it. I'm able to get it because we still have a diver in my family; my sister is still a part of my diving team and still exporting it.

WHAT ARE YOUR FAVORITE WAYS TO PREPARE IT?
There are so many. One of the ways that I like to eat it I call *playero*. It's just some sauce and lemon—Salsa Huichol, to be precise, with a little mustard and soy sauce. I often leave some of the seawater around the urchin, too. It's the urchin's juice, and it's definitely one of the best parts.

HOW DO YOU LIKE TO EAT SEA URCHIN?
I like it with just a bit of lime.

WERE YOU A CHEF IN ADDITION TO A DEEP-SEA DIVER?
When I was working on the tuna ship, I was a chef. I would also do work repairing deep-sea vessels. We repaired 1,200-ton ships. I began diving after that. I was working very hard because I had my daughters to support.

ARE ALL OF YOUR CUSTOMERS FAMILIAR WITH SEA URCHIN?
Most of my customers love sea urchin, but I say it's like the Bible: It's not for everyone. Sea urchin isn't for everyone—only for very special people.

*DO YOU HAVE A PREFERENCE FOR
SHELLFISH FROM THE SEA OF CORTEZ
VERSUS THE PACIFIC?*
Yes, the Pacific. It's better quality, because of the cold
water temperatures. It's where abalone, sea urchin,
and everything else that's good comes from. All of the
sea urchin that I serve comes from the coast just south
of Tijuana. That entire region is teeming with it, all
the way from Las Palomas to Alaska.

*THERE ARE SOME FISHING RESTRICTIONS
FOR SHELLFISH IN THE AREA. ARE THERE
ANY FOR SEA URCHIN?*
There's a ban on sea urchin harvesting during a four-
month period, from February to July. During that
time, I sell frozen urchin that's not nearly as good. It
has a different flavor; and I usually cook it with white
wine and oregano.

Sea Urchin Ceviche

250 g *(2 medium-sized) sea urchins*

150 g *(½ cup) diced tomatoes, seeds and pulp removed*

50 g *(¼ cup) sweet onion, such as Vidalia*

12 g *(2 tbsp) chopped cilantro*

150 g *(1 medium-sized) avocado, loosely cut in cubes*

30 g *(2 tbsp) fresh lime juice (Mexican limes, if available)*

0.5 g *(a pinch) sea salt to taste*

Prep time: 15 mins
Assembly time: 5 mins
Serves 2

1. Carefully cut off the top of each sea urchin making sure to discard any shell that might have broken loose and mixed with the urchin. With a paring knife, scoop and detach the urchin from the shell. Set aside and refrigerate.

2. Combine tomatoes, onion, cilantro, lime juice, and sea salt in a medium-sized bowl.

3. Gently mix in avocado, combining carefully so the avocado maintains its shape.

4. Take sea urchin out of the fridge and lay in strips on a plate, while minimizing overlap.

5. Top with vegetable mixture, and serve.

BENITO MOLINA

MANZANILLA, ENSENADA
31.85944 ° N, 116.63256 ° W

Before chef Benito Molina and his wife Solange Muris opened their first restaurant, Manzanilla, abalone and geoduck, native to nearby waters, were delicacies enjoyed by people all over the world—but not really at restaurants in Ensenada. The couple had a lightbulb moment: The local products available were fresher and better tasting than anything they were importing, so why not use them? Almost 15 years later, Molina is a renowned chef and television personality, while Manzanilla is credited with pioneering world-class dining in coastal Ensenada. It is also considered to be one of the restaurants shifting the tides of contemporary Mexican cooking.

WHEN DID YOU START COOKING?
I always liked being in the kitchen as a kid. My grandmother and mother are from Campeche, so I experienced extraordinary cooking in my house. I was always there watching.

Growing up, I wanted to be a marine biologist, so I could live in the sea. My parents sent me to military school in Lexington, Missouri. The worst food I've ever eaten in my life was there. And in the midst of this, I thought, "Okay, think, what's the most sophisticated thing I can do to get away from this horrible place?" There was a Maxim's de Paris in Mexico City. One night we ate there, and my mother's husband sat near a Frenchman, the chef of the King of Morocco. The next time we went, we spoke with the manager, who said that if I wanted to work some holidays there to see if I liked it, I would be welcome.

DID YOU GO?
I worked on the floor of Maxim's for one summer when I was 15. I remember the white collars and the gold buttons. I basically placed butter and served water. But it was amazing, because it was super-sophisticated: There were violins playing and waiters were all in tuxedos and tails. But there was a corridor with two doors, and when you opened the second door, there was fire and there were hilarious insults flying around. I thought, "Wow, those guys are having way more fun back there."

WHAT ABOUT MILITARY SCHOOL?
I never went back. My parents sent me to a school in Ojai, California. That's how I came to Ensenada for the first time; some of my friends there were from Ensenada and they invited me to come here with them. We weren't 21 yet, so we couldn't drink in the U.S., but here we could drink and do whatever we wanted. Those were incredible parties.

This was in the '80s, and I was very confused. I thought I wanted to be an economist, so I worked at a bank. Until one day, it hit me: I wanted to work in the back at Maxim's. I quit my job at the bank, dropped out of school, and went to work at Maxim's in the kitchen.

HOW DID IT GO AT MAXIM'S?
I was really lucky because the chef didn't speak Spanish. He was new, and I was the only one who spoke French. So I was promoted to be his assistant very quickly. The first day in the Maxim's kitchen, I said to myself, "This is what I'm going to do forever."

HOW LONG WERE YOU THERE FOR?
One year. But after that, I decided I had to go to school. My parents really loved that one: I was going to quit studying economics to become a chef. I wanted to go to France, but I learned that French chefs don't study at culinary schools, really. They go through public training. That is, they start training from age 16 at public high schools and have final exams where they have to memorize recipes. It's actually really hard.

What I found was great for me: a program at the New England Culinary Institute in Vermont. The school had four or five restaurants open to the public, and when I studied there, there were only seven alumni per chef. It was a restaurant where the chef was in charge and ultimately responsible, but the students cooked. That's how you learn to cook: by cooking.

SO THAT'S WHERE YOU LEARNED?
Well, before culinary school, I did another important

thing: I decided to work on a tuna fishing boat with the father of one of my Ensenada friends. I called him and told him, "I want to work with your dad on the boat." My friend laughed and said, "This fucking city boy is crazy." But he told me to go to La Paz, because that's where the boats were. His uncle took one look at me and told me I was crazy. He completely ignored me. I called my friend back, and he asked, "Are you actually serious? It's not a little thing. The boat has enough fuel and food to leave the shore for three months. Once it leaves, you're stuck." I did two trips; The first consisted of an entire month without once touching land.

WHAT WAS IT LIKE BEING ON THE BOAT?
I was washing the bathrooms, sinks, and kitchen. I also helped them fish. It was a ship with a 900-ton capacity for tuna and a helicopter landing pad on top. It had six speedboats and a giant contraption to pull the nets. It was definitely an experience.

That's where I learned about tuna. Part of the reason I wanted to do it in the first place was because I wanted to see how truthful they were about the dolphins. There are usually two guys in a small boat hitting the water, scaring the dolphins to get away. That's part of what I did. It turned out to be incredible. They really did everything they could to save the dolphins, like everything humanly possible.

WHAT AN EXPERIENCE.
That was the first trip. The second trip lasted a month and a half. Everything that gets into the net that is not tuna is for the "turkey." Except *el pavo*, was me—the bottom of the bottom—so that when we arrived at the port, we could sell fish and earn more money because they barely paid us. I got to the port in Acapulco with three sacks of fish and shark fin. That gave me 5,000 pesos I used to party. I went to cooking school after that.

WHAT DID YOU DO AFTER COOKING SCHOOL?
From there, I worked in Brittany, France, in a tiny little hotel by the sea. There were live lobsters, live crabs, everything. Then I worked in Boston at Olives, because at that moment, all my training had been 100 percent French, and my view of the kitchen was completely French. That totally Italian style made me see things differently.

I was interviewed at Olives by this sleeveless guy with tattoos wearing pink clogs around the kitchen. I thought, "Holy shit, what is this?" The chef looked like he was 15, had a broken leg, and I thought, "Did I come to the circus? This would never happen in a French kitchen." The restaurant didn't accept reservations. The reception was all glass and the kitchen all open, and people were standing in line. Speed is one of the most important things you learn when you cook in the United States. Because nowhere else in the world are people spinning tables that quickly.

THAT WAS YOUR FIRST IMPRESSION? DID YOU STAY?
When service was over, a waiter arrived and put pitchers of margaritas on the kitchen counter. I thought, "What is this? Where am I?" And they told me that if I wanted the job, it was mine, congratulations. I stayed there, and it completely changed my mind about cooking. Honestly, it was the best thing that happened to me.

WHEN DID MANZANILLA OPEN?
We opened July 31, 2000 and just passed the 15-year mark last week. Alex Atala and Enrique Olvera came to cook for the 15-year anniversary.

HOW WOULD YOU DESCRIBE YOUR COOKING THERE?
Above all, it's ingredient-driven cuisine. We work solely with local ingredients. Since Manzanilla opened, we've had live abalone on the menu. The wine has always been local wine from the nearby vineyards of Valle de Guadalupe. That's always been the idea: using things from the market and fresh products from the sea like oysters and mussels. I really like the sea.

WHAT DO YOU MEAN?
I was born in Mexico City, and I always wondered why people didn't live next to the sea. So, when I got a job offer to come to Ensenada to work, I took it.

WHEN WAS THAT?
I came here with Hugo D'Acosta 19 years ago. I worked for four years in Santo Tomás, where they processed wine. When I got to Santo Tomás, my cooking style was different from what it is today because I had so many other influences. I didn't know Ensenada products yet. Back then, absolutely no one

consumed ingredients from Ensenada in Mexico City, with one exception: canned abalone. Other than that, nothing. Nowadays, Ensenada cooking is in style all over Mexico. Ensenada ingredients can be found everywhere. But it was a lot of work to get to this point, and it took a lot of time. Back then, there was lots of food here, but it was all exported.

TO WHERE?
To China, California, Japan, the U.S., and Europe. Back then, we were talking to local producers and telling them we couldn't compete economically with the bulk they were sending to the United States, but they just didn't have clients here who could test the local products. At the time, there really was no restaurant using local products.

HOW DID IT GROW FROM THERE?
In that part of the story, Pablo Ferrer from El Sargazo appears. He is an oceanographer from the local university here who worked weekends in La Embotelladora Vieja, which was the name of the best-known restaurant in Santo Tomás. At one of the wine harvesting festivals—*La Vendimia*—the chef at the Four Seasons in Mexico City came. When he saw the spectacular swordfish we have in Ensenada, he began to ask why there was none of that in Mexico City. Pablo Ferrer was in the kitchen and heard that, so he started selling swordfish to the Four Seasons. That's how the the most important seafood relationships in Baja California began. Today, all the chefs buy from El Sargazo.

WHAT ARE THE BEST INGREDIENTS IN ENSENADA?
There are many things, but definitely the sea is, I would say, the most important ingredient of all, because everything comes out of it. The microclimate here, like in the wine country of Valle de Guadalupe, would not be possible without the sea. What happens here is that there are currents coming from Alaska, upwelling currents, that surface in this bay. That's why the water is so cold and the seafood is so good. The cold air gets into Valle and creates a Mediterranean-like microclimate.

ON YOUR MENU, IT SAYS "CULTIVATED ABALONE." WHAT DOES THAT MEAN?
There is a farm cultivating abalone in Eréndira, about an hour and a half south of Ensenada. For a single abalone to reach commercial size, it takes four years.

And an abalone at four years still has a small shell. If you talk to people who grew up here, like me 30 years ago, I ate huge abalone—*huge*. But after an influx of immigrants from Asia and elsewhere, we've almost run out of that kind of abalone in Ensenada.

IS THERE ANY SORT OF PROTECTION FOR ABALONE?
It is carefully protected now. There are cooperatives that help, but the abalone are very delicate in certain places, such as La Isla de Cedros. Cultivated abalone is an option. Obviously wild abalone has amazing flavor; probably one of the best things I've ever eaten in my life. When you put a whole abalone over a wood-burning fire, it's just crazy. But wild abalone is not always available. We can have the cultivated variety all the time. Cultivated abalone is tiny, and has a milder flavor than wild abalone. But it's still very good. I've had abalone on the menu since we first opened the restaurant.

One interesting thing about abalone is that it feeds on algae. Abalone does not pollute anything in the aquaculture because it acts as a filter. Oysters, mussels, and clams all act as water filters, feeding on microorganisms. They help reduce pollution; it's one of the reasons they're considered sustainable.

THERE'S ALSO A LOT OF GEODUCK ON YOUR MENU.
Yes, we also call it "the generous one" or "the well-hung clam." It's incredible and interesting. I tried it for the first time when I was working in Boston, but I never imagined that it existed in Mexico. Have you been to the market yet?

NO, NOT YET.
That's one of the things that's changed since I came to Ensenada. Now in the *Mercado Negro* [Ensenada's main fish market], there are tanks with live geoduck and other things. There is a giant fish vendor that's dedicated to exporting live fish to Los Angeles, so they are completely focused on having spectacular product. I say that a lot, but this is the only place in Mexico where you can see something like that. You go to a fish store here, just four blocks away, and it'll have live abalone, two or three species of live fish, and live lobster.

That such a small place like Ensenada has a range of things like that is what makes this location important. *////*

So many things come together here—olive oil, wine—that the work of a chef becomes much easier.

HOW HAS THE DINING SCENE CHANGED HERE OVER THE YEARS?
It has changed radically. When I arrived, there wasn't really anything. There was the famous El Rey Sol, but really just that. Obviously we had extraordinary carts, like Sabina [Bandera]'s La Guerrerense, but there was no formal restaurant that used 100 percent local produce. We were lucky to be the first. And, shortly after, Jair [Téllez] opened Laja.

HOW WOULD YOU DESCRIBE THE DINING IN ENSENADA THEN?
There was also a restaurant called Kaia, which was run by Basque owners. It was perhaps the best option we had. Because of the tuna fishing and a few other things, there is also a little Spanish influence in Ensenada.

The food here, above all else, is food for the home. In other words, the local fish and other ingredients weren't sent to restaurants here. What some people don't understand is that it's a very small place and the seasons affect us. In winter in Ensenada, there's not much tourism. With wine, it's starting to pick up. But then the flight tickets become expensive and hotels and restaurants tell you they're full.

SO, CULINARY TOURISM IS GROWING HERE, BUT SLOWLY.
One of the problems we do have is low hotel capacity. It's difficult because during the low season, the hotels mostly sit vacant, and are completely sold out during the Vendimia.

We've had a recent string of bad luck, too. First, the economic crisis of 2008; then, scares of violence from things that were happening elsewhere in Mexico; and then, swine flu.

IS MANZANILLA YOUR ONLY RESTAURANT?
We have another restaurant in Valle de Guadalupe called Silvestre. It's only open during the high season and on weekends. There's no electricity in the kitchen, just wood. No gas either. We're lucky we opened the first restaurant like it. It's a restaurant in the middle of a vineyard surrounded by olive trees with a 180-degree view of the vineyard.

Yellowtail Tiradito with Capers and Strawberries

5 g *(1 tsp) extra virgin olive oil*

120 g *fresh sushi grade yellowtail (alternatively, black cod or rockfish can be used)*

48 g *(4 small) local strawberries cut into small squares*

10 g *(2 ½ tsp) capers*

5 g *(2 tbsp) fresh ginger, finely chopped*

5 g *(2 tbsp) serrano pepper, finely chopped, seeds removed*

0.5 g *(a pinch) pasilla chile powder (can substitute any other chile)*

4 g *(1 tsp) soy sauce*

4 g *(1 tsp) raspberry vinegar*

1 *handful of greens from the garden (such as frisée, arugula, mizuna, cress)*

Prep time: 15 min
Assembly time: 5 min
Serves 2

1. Coat plate with olive oil.

2. Slice the fish very thin, and lay slices on the plate.

3. Add the strawberries, capers, fresh chopped ginger, and serrano pepper.

4. Season with chile powder, soy sauce, and vinegar. Top with the greens from the garden.

5. Optional: Add additional olive oil to taste.

SABINA BANDERA

LA GUERRERENSE, ENSENADA
31.86145 ° N, 116.62309 ° W

In between questions (and sometimes while answering them), the vivacious and affable Sabina Bandera doles out *cocteles*, *ceviches*, and *tostadas* topped with one of her dozen signature salsas. Her Ensenada stand, Mariscos La Guerrerense, serves some of the freshest fish in Baja, and with added flair, thanks to the unexpected flavor combinations her homemade salsas—a terrific peanut one, in particular—bring to the plate. Put on the map by Anthony Bourdain, Rick Bayless, and Benito Molina, among other chefs and television personalities, Mariscos La Guerrerense embodies the perfect blend of phenomenal shellfish, relaxed no-tables vibes, and satisfied ambition.

WHAT IS LA GUERRERENSE?
La Guerrerense was founded in 1960 by my in-laws. My mother and father-in-law—may they rest in peace—are from Guerrero and Tulancingo. I arrived here in Ensenada in 1976, so I guess 39 years ago, with my husband. We were visiting our in-laws for our honeymoon, and we're still here today.

DID YOU EVER WORK IN RESTAURANTS BEFORE THAT?
Nope, never. My father was a rancher and farmer. I made cow dairy products—cream, cheese, cottage cheese—and did some planting. I was always handling food from the farm with my mother, but I had never done anything with seafood.

WHEN YOU FIRST ARRIVED TO ENSENADA, WHAT WAS IT LIKE?
It has changed a lot since then. The *Mercado Negro* fish market was in a different location; it's also been remodeled. In my neighborhood, there were only five houses. And there used to be a ton of cattle at the market. That's where I would buy milk to turn into cheese. In the evenings, I would make cream, cheese, and *requesón*. When I first arrived, I was selling homemade cheese.

YOU HAD A CHEESE BUSINESS?
I'd make cheese in the evenings only, really. Because I came here to work during the days, I'd make cream and cheese to sell to the neighbors after hours.

NO MORE CHEESE THESE DAYS?
No more cheese. It's purely seafood these days. There's no more super fresh milk because the cattle ranch closed, and now the milk comes from very far away. I used to really enjoy making cheese, though.

ONE OF THE BEST THINGS ABOUT YOUR TOSTADAS IS THE WAY YOU INCORPORATE HOMEMADE SALSAS. WHAT'S THE STORY BEHIND THESE SALSAS?
I started doing that 13 years ago. I started with two sauces: a peanut one with smoked chiles that I created, and the one I now call the "mother-in-law" sauce because, well, my mother-in-law came up with the recipe.

I remember I used to store the peanut salsa—called *chilitos de mi jardín*—in Tupperware. Now I have a giant clay cauldron; that's how popular it's become. It's our most popular salsa, made with dried chiles, garlic, almonds, and peanuts. It goes very quickly. After those two sauces, little by little, I started inventing more and more until, before I knew it, I had 16 different sauces. Until now, that is: I'm working on another sauce with passion fruit. I'll let you know how that one turns out.

ARE THE SALSAS SOMETHING FROM GUERRERO? YOU DON'T SEE THAT STYLE OF PREPARATION MUCH IN ENSENADA.
Yes, it's not from here. It's something from my hometown. We have a lot of hot chiles in Guerrero, and we make a lot of different salsas there. Some are better for meat, others for shellfish.

NOW YOUR SALSAS ARE KNOWN WORLDWIDE.
I took these salsas to Singapore. The people there loved them. But we're not distributing outside of Mexico yet. We want to, but we have to get the paperwork done first. There's so much paperwork.

WHERE WILL YOU SELL THEM?
We're first working on selling salsas in the U.S. My daughter actually just brought home a certification sheet that gives us the right to distribute.

HOW DOES IT WORK WHEN YOU TRAVEL? DO YOU BRING THE SHELLFISH WITH YOU?
In Singapore, I just brought the sauces and about 2,500 *tostadas*.

IS THERE A DIFFERENCE IN THE QUALITY OF THE INGREDIENTS, FOR EXAMPLE, BETWEEN THE CLAMS HERE IN MEXICO AND THE ONES YOU'VE USED IN THE UNITED STATES OR SINGAPORE?
In Singapore, they didn't give me clams; it was only shrimp, octopus and scallops then. There was some crab, too. I made them a fish *ceviche* with some crab and shrimp *tostadas*, with octopus on top to give it the Guerrerense touch. It tastes very different there; it lacks a sort of natural seasoning and flavor.

Sometimes, when I'm in the U.S., it's difficult to get sea urchin. In that case, I bring sea urchin stew so people can try some.

HOW HAVE THINGS CHANGED SINCE YOU FIRST STARTED?
Customers started coming little by little. Benito Molina really helped to promote us in the beginning, back in 2000. He went on TV and said, "Go to La Guerrerense and eat with Sabina. Try this, try that." Benito, Aquiles Chávez, Enrique Olvera—I have a great relationship with these guys, and I love them all very much. I also owed a lot of thanks in the beginning to Anthony Bourdain and Rick Bayless, who sent people my way.

IS THAT WHEN THINGS REALLY PICKED UP?
Yes, that's right. In 2000, we appeared in Mexico's *Reforma* because of Benito. Then we appeared in the in-flight magazines on Aeroméxico and Mexicana Airlines. We appeared in *San Diego Reader* in 2003; then the *New York Times* shortly after. May all the world come, *ojalá*.

BEFORE 2000, WERE YOUR CUSTOMERS MOSTLY LOCALS?
Yes, back then it was mostly Mexicans—rarely anyone from the United States. Locals still make up the majority, but we see people from all over now; Europe and the United States, especially. People come from Poland saying, "I saw you on TV with Anthony Bourdain!" I'm always shocked when I hear this.

IS THERE ANY DIFFERENCE BETWEEN WHAT LOCALS AND FOREIGNERS ORDER?
Not really. But sometimes the ones who don't really speak Spanish just order sea urchin.

DO YOU HAVE A FAVORITE TOSTADA YOURSELF?
I really like the one with sea urchin and chocolate clams, because the sea urchin salsa is warm, and the clam is cold and fresh. I like that contrast. Then I add the *chilitos de mi jardín* salsa, which gives it the final exotic touch. I'm always changing what I eat here, though.

WHAT DO YOU USUALLY EAT AT HOME?
On my day off, I'll eat crab, *pescado zarandeado* that my husband makes, fried fish, or maybe some lobsters when they're in season. But I almost always eat seafood. I love it. It's very easy to get great fish here. It's so fresh.

LA GUERRERENSE IS A STREET STAND, BUT THE FLAVORS CAN COMPETE WITH MANY OF THE WORLD'S GREAT RESTAURANTS.
We have no seats, no tables. I tell people, "Standing only, so you can eat better!" Sometimes, people sit on the floor, or in one of the plastic seats we have. I like when people come to eat my food, and they know where they are. We don't need tables or tablecloths. The people that come here come here to eat. That's it.

Soon, though, I want to open a small seafood restaurant with tables. On Fridays and Saturdays, I'm going to make *pozole*. I'll maybe also make a *mole* in the style of where I'm from on Sundays.

ARE THERE REGULARS THAT COME SO OFTEN, YOU KNOW THEIR ORDERS BY HEART?
Of course. Benito Molina always orders the *tostada* with sea urchin and clam. Actually, he invented that recipe in 1993, when he first started coming. Enrique Olvera, too. He always orders the *tostada* with sea urchin and clam, or sometimes he orders clam just in the shell. Solange, Benito's wife, loves clam in its shell with a fish *ceviche*.

I more or less always know who orders what.

Baja-Style Pismo Clam Ceviche

3 large white clams

200 g (1 medium-sized) white onion

340 g (2 medium-sized) tomato

80 g (1 bunch) of cilantro

255 g (3 medium-sized) limes

0.5 g (1 pinch) sea salt

200 g (1 medium-sized) avocado

Prep time: 10 min
Assembly time: 5 min
Serves 1

1. Open and clean clams by removing the clams' stomachs.

2. Cut meat from clam in small 1 cm cubes.

3. Dice the onion, tomatoes, and cilantro into small pieces.

4. Combine clams with vegetable mixture and add juice from 3 limes.

5. Season with salt to taste.

6. Garnish with sliced avocado. Lay avocado on top of clams.

Scallop Aguachile

250 g (10 large) scallops

220 g (1 medium-sized) red onion

340 g (1 medium-sized) cucumber, peeled, seeds removed

750 g (10 small) Mexican limes

0.5 g (1 pinch) of dried chile de árbol powder (can substitute in other chile powder)

10 lemons

0.5 g (1 pinch) salt

0.5 g (1 pinch) pepper

Prep time: 15 min
Assembly time: 5 min
Serves 2

1. Thinly slice scallops (3 mm thick).

2. Cut the red onion into thin slices.

3. Finely chop the cucumber.

4. Place scallops on a plate and top with onions and cucumber. Add the lime juice, the dried chile de árbol powder, and salt and pepper to taste.

5. Let sit for 5 minutes.

DREW DECKMAN

DECKMAN'S EN EL MOGOR, VALLE DE GUADALUPE
32.03560 ° N, 116.60163 ° W

Chef Drew Deckman is a fisherman, but you might never know it from his pedigree. Over the course of a decade in France, Switzerland, and Germany, Deckman worked with some of the food world's most respected chefs, including Paul Bocuse, and earned his restaurant, Restaurant Vitus in Reinstorf, Germany, a Michelin star. Yet all he wanted was to be near the sea. He thought about moving to Hawaii, Cape Town, Key West, and Tahiti, but ultimately settled in Baja, where the quality of the food matched the quality of the sea.

Good choice: Now you can find him cooking over an open fire at Deckman's en El Mogor, a restaurant in a lush vineyard in Mexico's Valle de Guadalupe. We could think of worse offices.

HOW DID DECKMAN'S GET STARTED?
When we opened this place in July 2012, we thought this was just going to be somewhere we were going to come and hang out for a couple months. It didn't have to be a viable business for us, because we had a place in Cabo that was working. But we would close our place in Cabo in August and September anyway, because nobody's there in those months, so we figured why not come up here? This was just going to be where we would test recipes for the next season in Cabo—and a place to get away from the 115 degree heat.

HOW DID YOU FIRST CHOOSE TO COME UP TO VALLE DE GUADALUPE?
I've been working here in Valle in some capacity for at least the last seven years, and the general Baja state for nine. I was a culinary consultant for Hugo D'Acosta and worked with him at his wineries. He treats wine the same way you would treat any other ingredient, and wanted a culinary liaison between his winemakers and the finished wine.

WHAT KIND OF WORK DID YOU DO ON THE VINEYARDS?
My job with them really was two-fold. One, to just bang out their summer event and take care of all the food, but also, to really be that bridge between the winemaker, the wine, and the customer. I learned so much. But after doing that for a couple of years, I went back to Cabo in 2011, broke and tired, and said, "Sure, I can do that, but I don't have to work for somebody. I can do that self-employed." There wasn't much going on in Valle with restaurants yet. Diego Hernandez [from Corazón de Tierra] had not opened yet; he was just thinking about it.

HOW DID YOU GET FROM JUST AN IDEA TO ACTUALLY OPENING THE RESTAURANT?
Natalia Badan, the owner of El Mogor vineyard, is

really the matriarch of what's going on here. I just showed up and said, "Can I buy you a cup of coffee? I need some advice," essentially. I saw opening up here as a risk, but I still felt like I wanted to do it. I asked her what she thought. Her reaction was, "Won't you set up underneath my pine trees?"

WHY DO YOU THINK SHE GAVE YOU THAT VOTE OF CONFIDENCE?
I think she got the feeling that I was going to do something anyway. Why not with her? We went through this several-weekends-long process where we thought about feng shui. We sat here with bottles of wine, and tried to imagine where the grill should be and what the angle and perspective of the diner should be. Then I started designing the ship.

The idea was that there are no waiters, so the cooks were the waiters, and there's no differentiation between where the floor stops and the kitchen begins. The idea was that you had this interactive, pretension-free dining experience on one of the most traditional ranches in all of Valle. All of a sudden, we needed more seats and I needed to hire waiters. We liked that first year so much that we did six months the second year. The third year, I shut down Cabo, and came here full time.

HOW DID YOU FIRST END UP IN CABO?
My other gig is, I fish for a living—commercially, professionally, for sport, and also, for tournaments. I also work as a Divemaster. So when I was looking for somewhere in the world where I could cook and fish, I basically narrowed it down to five places: Key West, Tahiti, Cape Town, Kona, and Cabo.

I'd never been to any of them, other than Kona. But I identified five locations where food and fishing were of high-enough quality, but then I had to narrow it down depending on security, ease of access to the real world—but not too close—and mountains next to ocean. Key West was out, and Tahiti could sort of qualify.

HOW DID CABO WIN?
Because in Los Cabos, you have a shot at some sort of a billfish 365 days a year, which is cool. People here get swordfish, bluebacks, striped marlin, and recently, shortbill spearfish, which is normally only caught in Hawaii. Though, I guess the waters are changing. There's great tuna fishing here, too. Ten years ago, it was a no-brainer. The quality of food was pretty high then.

WHAT ABOUT NOW?
I think the Cabo offering has expanded, but I think the quality has gone down across the board.

WHY?
I think that the phenomenon of the all-inclusive tourist changes the way you have to do business in that kind of a market. It is pretty limiting. I would say that 85 percent of your guests in restaurants don't live in the Cabo area. That's not based on anything other than a gut feeling. Or, if they do own a home, they are not in Cabo year-round. When you get somebody who's really transient, I think it reduces the number of people who really care about the origin of food they're eating, which is really important to me.

Consuming local and promoting local producers, even though it may a little more expensive, also means maybe you only get carrots for two months. Or that there are tomatoes in the winter but not in the summer. But to meet hotel standards, you have to have strawberries on the breakfast buffet. And you have to have certain things that don't necessarily grow regionally. Then there's also a tipping point of your volume—a small artisan market can't always provide large enough quantities.

WHO WAS THE CABO TRAVELER WHEN YOU WERE THERE?
It was a budget-free environment, and it was wild. The kind of people that were coming there, the kind of people that were buying memberships, the kind of houses that were being built, the kind of food that people wanted to eat. People cared about where their food was from. I think, probably in 2008, when the economy changed a lot, there were close to 200 spec houses that cost $3,000,000 left standing in the Cabo area.

Hotels stopped being built. And then the storm [Hurricane Odile in 2014], I think, helped the market reach its ultimate bottom. Whatever little bit was still hanging on, whatever little bit of recovery may have been coming economically, the storm just eliminated anybody that didn't have huge bags of money.

WHERE DID YOU GROW UP?
I was born in Washington D.C., but I grew up in Georgia and went to high school about an hour south of Atlanta in Peachtree City, Georgia. It took me a while to figure out what I wanted to do, and I'm still trying to figure it out. I went to the U.S. Merchant Marine Academy by Kings Point, New York, for my first year of college, which was interesting. I figured out really, really quickly that neither was I built for the military nor was the military built for me. I left Kings Point after a little over a year and thought, "I'm going to be a dentist like my dad." That lasted for about ten minutes.

WHAT DID YOU SETTLE ON THEN?
I took some introductory philosophy courses at Georgia Southern University and thought those were really cool. The next quarter, I took a few more and started to ignore whatever my normal coursework was. By the third quarter, I took all philosophy courses. At this point, my dad's asking questions like, "I thought you were going to be a dentist."

I transferred a bunch of times, and was very distracted. But I eventually graduated from Rhodes College in Memphis, Tennessee, a small private liberal arts college, with a degree in philosophy. There's not much you can do with philosophy, but I thought I wanted to be a professional baseball umpire. I was going to go to umpire school. That didn't work out. I thought about being a lawyer, too.

WHAT WAS YOUR FIRST JOB OUT OF COLLEGE?
My first gig out of college landed me at Enterprise Rent-a-Car. I was in Tampa, Florida, and somehow I decided at that point that I was going to be a Enterprise lifer, and that I was born to be part of the Enterprise family. They were expanding to the Dakotas and Montana, so this was my opportunity

to really move up, and eventually be a branch and regional manager. You know, the things that go through your head when you're 21 years old. I moved from Tampa to Bismarck, North Dakota, in October. But a few months in, I woke up with this epiphany one morning that I wanted to go back to the kitchen and cook for a living. So I moved back home to my parents' house and cooked for about a year in Atlanta, and then went to Europe. I thought I was going for six months, but I stayed ten years.

YOU'VE COOKED IN—GERMANY, SWITZERLAND, FRANCE, HAWAII, MEXICO, AND OTHER COUNTRIES—HOW HAS THAT INFLUENCED YOUR COOKING STYLE?
I don't see myself as a chef. I say this every chance I get, but to me, chefs are the guys I worked for in Europe who have had three Michelin stars for 40 years, one after another. I'm an ingredient facilitator, maybe. Find what's best in the market and I'll try to not screw it up before I give it to you. We have the real advantage here that we produce a lot of our own food. We didn't plant the tomato plants, for example; they just magically appeared.

SO, DO YOU USE ALL LOCAL INGREDIENTS?
I still think commercially produced local ingredients are better than organically produced ingredients that come from a long way away. By burning how many thousands of calories of petroleum fuel to bring organic lettuce from someplace else, it sort of loses its organic karma. But we have lambs and Charolais cattle here, along with bees we keep for honey. The idea is to be as vertically integrated as possible. If you can produce it, produce it. If you can't or choose not to, at least buy it from your neighbor who's doing it the right way. There is some stuff—cinnamon, for example, which doesn't grow in Mexico very well. But when we use vanilla, it's from Veracruz; not from Tahiti or someplace else.

Probably my favorite place in all my travels was Provence in the south of France. Just being able to walk up the hill and pick abundant herbs and mushrooms. This is the only place that I've seen equal that.

IS YOUR TECHNIQUE SOMETHING THAT YOU LEARNED IN GERMANY OR FRANCE, OR IS IT A MIXTURE OF BOTH?
I think your palate can change over the course of your culinary career, but I think your hands get imprinted with a technique or style as you're starting to learn the way to hold your knife or cut things. You can learn, but your baseline is the imprinting. For me, I cut my teeth with French chefs in Geneva. But they had a south of France palate, so they used olive oil instead of cream and butter. Or they would fry a steak in rendered kidney fat as opposed to frying it in butter.

But my goal has always been to assimilate. I wouldn't go to Monterrey and say, "Let's open a French restaurant." For me, it's important to integrate what's local, and then, by default, a lot of the flavors in your kitchen change. If you work off a concept as opposed to recipes, but one of those ingredients is not in the marketplace, the recipe doesn't work.

HOW DO YOU COOK NOW?
We cook a lot with fire. You can't get away from the fire—and we're not trying to—but what's really important for us is that we choose wisely the type of wood we use. If you use hickory, mesquite, or olive, it's pungent enough to build on the palate. By the end of the meal, everything you've eaten—even if you sauté something in the pan, it's being sautéed on a wood fire—the smoke is still painting the dish. Even our coffee and ice cream: We cook the base for the ice cream over the wood fire. Everything is smoky.

YOU'VE BEEN IN MEXICO NOW FOR OVER TEN YEARS. WHAT HAVE YOU LEARNED FROM MEXICAN CUISINE OR WHAT YOU'VE SEEN IN BAJA?
When I was in high school, I spent three summers in the Yucatán. The first year was a missionary thing, back when I believed in something. Then the next two summers, I went by myself backpacking. I didn't speak Spanish or any of the indigenous languages. I never saw it that way, but if I look back, it's pretty clear, I think, that I was heading for the kitchen or the kitchen had chosen me.

WHAT DO YOU MEAN?
I think the future of Mexican food is any food produced with Mexican ingredients. We're planting *papalo*, for instance. As the presence of Mexican cuisine in the world increases—and it is increasing exponentially—it's really challenging to communicate tradition and history.

You could come to me and sit down and say, "I want to tell you about the *mole* my grandmother made." But if I don't know your grandmother,

or never actually ate the *mole*, it's a story that's interesting, but for the growth of a cuisine globally, I think it's limiting to rely on that sort of tradition as your vehicle for communication. But everybody understands origin of ingredient. I could tell you about a certain chile that was grown in Oaxaca and why it's important, the guys that are growing it, their tradition behind it, and some of the typical dishes built behind that chile. That's so much easier to communicate than grandma's *mole*.

YOU'VE TRAVELED AND COOKED ALL OVER THE WORLD. WHAT'S SPECIAL ABOUT VALLE DE GUADALUPE?

Obviously for me, there's no secret that I like the ocean. For me, anywhere in Baja is amazing, because the ocean here is world-class. Like, World Class with capital W and capital C. We are talking about superior oceans.

Look at where we are right now, because that answers a lot of the question "Why am I here?" Even the camera doesn't really do it justice. I've had worse offices—that's for sure. I like this juxtaposition of being on a ranch and eating the best oysters you ever had in your life. Like, how can that happen? Abalone, spotted prawns, and spider crab all being harvested within three hours from where we are. Most places in the United States travel a lot more than that. So I think that is really special when we talk about just ingredients.

Second is wine. As I've moved around the world a little bit, I've noticed that the quality of life is better in a place that produces wine. Maybe it's the weather? I don't know what it is, but the culture around wine is elevated. The culinary IQ is higher. The general appreciation of what's happening is better and I don't think it's because everybody is drunk.

WHAT DO YOU MEAN BY ELEVATED CULTURE?

It all just slows down a little bit. People spend more time at the table. It's also cool because you know lots of people who make wine. You sit down and it's like, "Have you tried this?" Now there are 15 bottles on the table and we're all trying what's new.

Beer is another ingredient that's really good in Baja. We're right next to San Diego, which is arguably the number one artisan beer city in the United States right now. San Diego is wild. Every day there's something new there, and every day the beer is better than it was the day before. There are about 35 artisan breweries here that are producing really good beer. Some are legal; some aren't. That's another nice thing: There's not a whole lot of vigilance here. They don't ask for tax stickers and things like that all the time. The northwest part of Baja is really a special place.

YOU MENTIONED EARLIER THAT YOU TRY TO ASSIMILATE WITH YOUR SURROUNDINGS. WHAT HAS THAT PROCESS BEEN LIKE FOR YOU IN BAJA?

I'm not Mexican, obviously. And even though I'm now a permanent resident, I will always be a *gringo*. But I think it's really important that whenever I speak to people about what I do, I always talk about the destination. I talk about the producer. I talk about drinking Mexican wines, about being responsible in your food choices.

But you still get this conversation of "Hey, why don't you invite Drew to this event that's promoting Baja?" followed by "Oh, but he's not from here." Either way, I really believe that if the destination wins, everybody does. We're on this bus together. One big-ass submarine is so much more efficient than 137 different ones at depth.

Oysters with Cucumber and Pink Peppercorn Mignonette

1 g (1 tsp) pink peppercorns, ground

40 g (1 small) shallot, finely diced

125 g (½ cup) red wine vinegar

12 Kumamoto oysters fresh, very cold

120 g (½ medium-sized) Persian cucumber, peeled, seeds removed, finely diced

30 g (2 tbsp) fish roe (such as trout roe)

150 g (½ cup) very coarse sea salt for decoration

3 g (a pinch) algae or herbs (such as salicornia) for decoration

14 g (1 tbsp) extra virgin olive oil

Prep time: 15 min
Assembly time: 5 min
Serves 2

PART I: MIGNONETTE

1. Mix peppercorn, shallot, and vinegar in a small bowl.

2. Set aside.

PART II: OYSTERS

1. Place the salt and algae decoration on a serving dish large enough to fit 12 oysters.

2. Shuck oysters to open.

3. Once open, place a few drops of mignonette to taste on each oyster. Add a pinch of diced cucumber.

4. Finish by placing one drop of olive oil and ½ tsp fish roe in each oyster.

Beet-Painted Abalone and Sea Urchin

240 g (1 cup) white vinegar

50 g (¼ cup) sugar

0.25 g (1 medium-sized) bay leaf

34 g (2 tbsp) sea salt

60 g (½ cup) water

340 g (1 large) large beet

300 g (1 bunch) baby beets

24 g (2 tbsp) extra virgin olive oil

13 g (1 tbsp) sherry vinegar

4 live abalone

100 g (½ small) white onion, julienned

1 g (1 sprig) thyme

8 pieces of sea urchin

50 g arugula leaves

2.5 g (1 tsp) pepper, fresh-ground

2 g (1 tsp) ground fennel seed

40 g (1 small) shallot, finely diced

115 g (1 medium-sized) Meyer lemon or fresh bergamote, to taste

Prep time: 24 hours
Cooking time: 1 hour
Serves 4

PART I: PICKLING BEETS

1. Boil the vinegar, sugar, bay leaf, 1 tbsp of salt, and water for 5 minutes.

2. Remove from heat and allow to cool to 135° F (57° C). In the meantime, slice 2 baby beets into approximately 1/16 inch pieces using a mandoline. Place into a medium-sized bowl.

3. When the vinegar mix reaches 135° F (57° C), pour over sliced beets in bowl. Let stand, covered, at room temperature for 24 hours, then refrigerate.

PART II: BEET "PAINT" SAUCE

1. Juice the large beet in a juicer

2. Place in a saucepan over medium heat. Reduce to ⅓ of the original volume.

3. Season with a pinch of salt to taste.

4. Strain and cool.

PART III: ROASTED BEETS

1. Wrap the baby beets in aluminum foil with a pinch of salt and 1 tbsp of olive oil.

2. Bake for one hour in oven pre-heated to 375°F.

3. Allow to cool. Peel beet and dice into small pieces.

4. Season with a pinch of salt and pepper, ½ of the sherry vinegar, a pinch of ground fennel seed, and 1 tsp of olive oil.

PART IV: BEET VINAIGRETTE

1. Combine one spoonful of the beet reduction, the remaining sherry vinegar, and 1 tsp of olive oil.

2. Set aside.

PART V: ROASTED ABALONE

1. Wrap the 4 abalone (closed, in their shells) with the onion, a pinch of thyme, and 1 tsp of olive oil in aluminum foil. Place in a wood-fired oven (or conventional oven at 400° F or 205° C) on high heat until the abalone can be removed from its shell without effort.

2. Allow to cool until you can handle them comfortably.

3. Clean the abalone by removing the stomach and beak.

4. Slice into paper thin slices, where slices do not overlap.

PART VI: TO ASSEMBLE

1. On four separate medium-sized plates, brush plate surface with the beet "paint".

2. Divide the abalone equally among the four plates. Season with a pinch of salt and pepper.

3. Place three slices of the pickled beets, along with roasted beet salad on each plate.

4. Place two pieces of the sea urchin on each plate. Top with the arugula leaves.

5. Grate some Meyer lemon or fresh bergamote over the top of each portion.

DIEGO HERNÁNDEZ

CORAZÓN DE TIERRA, VALLE DE GUADALUPE
32.03899 ° N, 116.65330 ° W

Ask Diego Hernández a question, and you'll almost certainly receive an astute, information-packed reply that reveals his encyclopedic knowledge of food and its context in Baja. He's been trained in prestigious kitchens, under chefs like Benito Molina and Enrique Olvera, but his heart lies with his own hyper-local restaurant, Corazón de Tierra, for which he grows most of his own vegetables in Valle de Guadalupe. A Baja native, Hernández is deeply invested in the region's cuisine, past and present, and has a few ideas for where it'll go next.

HOW WOULD YOU DESCRIBE CORAZÓN DE TIERRA?
We opened it in 2011. To me, it was like the sequel of a concept, because I opened my first restaurant in Tijuana in 2008.

WHAT WAS THAT RESTAURANT CALLED?
Its name was Uno. I was still at culinary school when we had the chance to open that place. At that particular moment in Mexico, a lot of my peers were starting to emerge from different parts of the country.

It's very difficult to talk about Mexican food as a whole, because Mexico is a very big country with so many different ecosystems, regions, ingredients, and cultures. That's what makes it interesting. Because when you talk about a dish—for example, *chiles en nogada*—it was made in a particular place, at a particular time, during a particular season. Food here responds to geography, but also, to culture.

It makes sense to make *chile en nogada* in September in Puebla. To make it elsewhere in January or November—buying a chile from Idaho and walnuts from I don't know where—doesn't make sense. That's the beauty of Mexican food.

HOW DOES THAT FACTOR INTO YOUR RESTAURANTS?
When we opened this restaurant, I really wanted to do food from Baja California. I grew up in Ensenada.

ARE YOUR PARENTS FROM HERE TOO?
My mom is from Mexico City, my dad is from Tampico, and his family is from Jalisco, but they moved to Ensenada in the 1950s. That's sort of the story of everyone around here.

WHAT DOES THAT MEAN FOR BAJA TRADITIONS?
We don't really have any old traditions. We don't have traditional recipe books. We don't have a lot of things that could make you say, "This is the food from Baja." But we have very, very good ingredients, and we have a culture. This culture is what we tried to represent in the restaurant.

HOW WOULD YOU DESCRIBE BAJA CULTURE?
Baja is a land of migrants, and there are a lot of people with a lot of different backgrounds. They all cook with the same ingredients but through the filter of their own cultures. At this precise moment, I think that's what Baja food is.

HOW DOES THAT PLAY OUT AT THE RESTAURANT?
When we were at the restaurant here in Valle de Guadalupe, I partnered with a farmer. We had a greenhouse here. But when I tried the carrots from my greenhouse, I realized how important the soil and the climate were. Because, even if it's local, it's not enough if the produce doesn't have that stamp of the local flavor. You can have local carrots in a greenhouse anywhere in the world and they will pretty much taste the same, because they don't have soil from where you're planting. The greenhouse carrots may be very beautiful, but they are not very tasty.

WHY DO YOU THINK THAT IS?
I think all living species have to be exposed to some kind of stress, or fight for their lives, in order to develop. Because, if you give everything to them, they just grow to be beautiful but with nothing on the inside.

HOW DOES THAT PLAY OUT HERE?
When you have a way of farming like this, where

plants are exposed to a hot or freezing climate, plants die because of natural selection. The ones that make it are plants that are very, very strong, and get a lot of their energy from the soil. It takes double the effort for them to keep living, and I believe a lot of flavor comes from that. Winemakers use that same philosophy.

HOW DO YOU FEEL ABOUT THE TERM "BAJA MED," OR THE IDEA OF BAJA MEDITERRANEAN CUISINE?
Places are definitely trying to develop this idea of *Baja Med*—ingredients that are grown locally with newly invented techniques. I mean, Baja Norte now has tons of olive oil and ingredients like that.

One of the things that I like about Baja so much is that Baja California wasn't even a state until the 1970s, so most people that live here are migrants from other parts of Mexico. It's become this patchwork of different areas of Mexico, all in one. So you can have great *birria* from Jalisco and great fish tacos, all in one place.

WHERE DOES CORAZÓN DE TIERRA FIT IN WITH THIS NEW IDEA OF BAJA MED COOKING AND WORKING WITH RECIPES FROM OTHER PARTS OF MEXICO?
Of course, I'm from a newer generation. My only job in my entire life has been cooking; I haven't done anything else. I wasn't even trained cooking traditional Mexican food. I was trained with very modern chefs—Mexican, all of them—in Mexico. I never traveled to Europe or the United States to do my training.

So I think that what we're doing is an example of how Mexican food has evolved over the years. I was trained by a generation that needed to travel to Europe or the United States to get the training, and then come back to Mexico and apply those techniques to Mexican ingredients. It was a sort of food syncretism.

WHAT DO YOU MEAN BY THAT?
In the beginning of the 1900s, I think, a lot of migrants from Asia, especially from China and Japan, moved to Baja. Many were trying to get into the United States, but then the Mexican government gave a lot of support to families from China to build the railroad in Mexicali. So fifty families from China moved to Mexicali to build the railroad, and more

people came after them. When the railroad was finished, they stayed to farm cotton. Chinese culture became part of the Mexicali culture, and, of course, Baja culture.

HAVE YOU PERSONALLY EXPERIENCED THAT?
My grandmother is from Guadalajara. When she moved to Ensenada with my dad, my father tells me she was cooking food from Jalisco but with a lot of ingredients from Baja. That's where the mix of cultures starts. She was doing *birria*, but if she didn't have lamb, she was maybe using clams or tuna, so *birria y atún* was born.

And that's very common. If you ask any family in Baja, "What do you eat?", you'll find things like that. In the Baja California pantry, you always have pasta, olive oil, and soy sauce, for example.

WHAT ABOUT TECHNIQUES?
In Mexican food, we have techniques that we haven't completely developed yet. I'm not talking just about Baja. I'm talking about Mexico in general. We are still learning, but the chef community in Mexico is very unified. We try as much to all be friends and share whatever we learn with each other.

DO YOU MEAN MODERN OR TRADITIONAL TECHNIQUES?
Everybody knows the modern techniques. You can Google everything, and it just shows up. But I think that we need to dig a little bit deeper into Mexico, because there are some techniques that we are so frequently used to that it's hard to think outside the box. Sometimes it's easier for non-Mexicans to see a technique and find different ways to apply it, because they don't have the huge weight of a culture that tells you that masa is for *tortillas* and *tamales*.

ARE THERE ANY TRADITIONAL TECHNIQUES THAT YOU USE REGULARLY?
We do *nixtamal* for corn. When we have corn, we make masa, too. When we don't, we buy it from the local *tortilleria*. We try to experiment. One of my cooks is from Oaxaca, so I'm always learning things from him. We've been so focused these years on finding useful ways to use everything that is here, and on changing the menu so often that almost all of the techniques are very easy. We haven't done a lot of technique exploration, but that's something that I have in my mind and that I'm trying to find

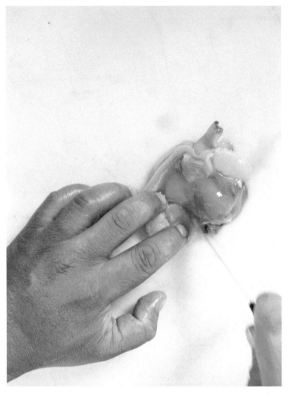

time to do. Because I think Mexican food is so, so interesting. You see a *chilpachole* as a soup, but maybe a *chilpachole* could be a technique. So I'm trying to figure out where the technique ends and the dish starts.

HOW DID YOU GET INTO COOKING?
I've always liked to eat, and even today, I like to eat more than I like to cook. I started cooking when I was studying business administration for a year in the local university. I wasn't really feeling it, and I liked food too much. My mom had a friend who was friends with Solange Muris, Benito Molina's wife. She commented, "Diego is thinking about studying cooking." And Solange recommended I hang out at the restaurant after school to see if I liked it.

HOW DID THAT GO?
I did it for, like, two weeks, and I loved it. I asked for a job position and they said, "You can come, but we can't pay you." I was fine with that. I dropped out of school and worked for them for a year and a half, unpaid. I got some tips, but I was still living at my parents' house, so it was easy. I had a place to sleep and eat. Really, it wasn't about the money. It was more about learning. Benito taught me how to hold the knife and everything.

WHEN WAS THAT?
That was at Manzanilla in 2001, and I was really into the idea of getting a normal education. You're supposed to finish high school, then go to university. But Benito told me, "No, this is a craft. You should learn first and then go to school." So I did it like that. I worked with Benito for a year and a half, then with Guillermo González Beristáin at Pangea for around three years, then at Pujol with Enrique for another year, and then I got into school in Tijuana. I was already cooking for six years when I got into school, and I finally understood what Benito told me because I had this background, so I was learning very quickly.

I have learned so much from other chefs in Mexico. It's a tight-knit community. The food we do here has changed over the years, and it has a lot to do with what you learn from friends and what you take in.

WHERE DOES THE MEDITERRANEAN FLAIR FIT INTO ALL OF THIS?
Wine and olive oil have been in Baja for a long time. It comes from the Spanish Crown; when it was New Spain, before it was Mexico. The vines were planted to make wine for the Catholic Church, and the olives were planted by the same missionaries that were planting the vines. It's been here for hundreds of years.

When the wine industry started producing Mexican wine, there were a few wineries but it's not like it was a movement. When they started to create the movement, they had to create food that goes along with Mexican wine from this region. They started doing the *Fiestas de la Vendimia*, and inviting chefs from Mexico City to come. When they got here and saw the quality of the ingredients that were here, they wanted to have that in Mexico City.

WHICH CHEFS ARE YOU REFERRING TO?
The characters that started all these things are people like Benito Molina, Bruno Oteiza, Hugo d'Acosta, and Pablo Ferrer. They all have some part in the story. I think that bringing fresh Mexican ingredients to the city started to change or shape the way we cook now all over Mexico.

WHAT DO YOU MEAN?
In early 2000, the best restaurants in Mexico were still Spanish, and before that, many were French. When Mexican chefs started owning Mexican restaurants, and had these ingredients available, is when everything started to take shape. People started coming to see what was new in Ensenada because food there was high-quality.

DO MANY TOURISTS COME HERE NOW?
Every season, we have more and more people from San Diego and Los Angeles coming, but it's because we've been sharing a lifestyle with people from Southern California for so many years. Even when the U.S. government said that Mexico was very dangerous—"Don't go to Mexico"—people that live right across the border used to come and say, "Let's give it another chance." But we also have a lot of first-time customers from San Diego and Los Angeles that have been telling us that this is their first time crossing the border in 15 or 20 years.

I do think people are starting to come again, but it's easier because they live so close by. From other parts of the United States, I think it's more difficult, because they don't know the lifestyle of this region. It's not like they used to come in the '80s to surf. It's different, and there's always a red alert like, "Don't go to Mexico." That's what we need to fight against most.

The other thing is infrastructure. We need roads, we need hotels, we need airports, and we need better public transportation.

IS THERE A DISH ON THE MENU THAT BEST REPRESENTS YOUR STYLE OF COOKING?
We always use shellfish, but it's not like we do it the same way all the time. It's more about the ingredient itself. Shellfish is very representative of Baja culture. You can see where nomads walked across the peninsula, because they used to eat shellfish and drop the shells along the way.

Those places, today called *concheros*, help archaeologists and anthropologists study people who were here thousands of years ago. They're very distinctive to the coast of Baja California and give us a window into what culture was like back then. For us, the *concheros* are as important as the pyramids are for Mexicans in central and southern Mexico. Usually the shellfish settle on beaches and mountains; and if you go to the mountains, you'll see all these paintings, tools, and houses the people used to have.

Shellfish has been part of our diet for hundreds and hundreds and hundreds of years, so at the restaurant, we put a lot of emphasis on using shellfish. And also, one of the techniques that we use all over the north of Mexico is a grill. For me, the use of smoke and shellfish is something that very representative of my cooking, but also of Baja cuisine.

Yellowtail Crudo with Radish, Tomatoes, and Lemon Verbena

2 g (5 thin slices) radish or turnip

60 g (¼ cup) rice wine vinegar

90 g (approx. 6 small) cherry tomatoes

60 g (5 thin bite-sized slices) yellowtail

20 g (approx. ⅛ medium-sized) cucumber, peeled, seeds removed

0.5 g (3 small) lemon verbena leaves

40 g (2 tbsp) extra virgin olive oil

0.5 g (1 pinch) salt

Prep time: 75 minutes
Assembly time: 15 minutes
Serves 1

1. Pickle the thin slices of radish or turnip by letting them sit in rice vinegar for one hour.

2. Grate 6 cherry tomatoes and place onto a plate to create a no-cook, instant tomato sauce.

3. Thinly slice the yellowtail and place on top of the tomato sauce.

4. Slice cucumbers and divide each slice into quarters. Add to the plate with the tomato and yellowtail.

5. Add one slice of radish or turnip for each piece of fish. If you have 5 pieces of fish, add 5 slices of radish.

6. Add a leaf of lemon verbena to each piece of fish.

7. Drizzle with olive oil and season with salt to taste.

Sunday Morning Oysters

7 *oysters*

15 g *(1 stalk with leaves) swiss chard*

56 g *(½ cup) queso fresco, grated*

35 g *(1 large strip) thick-cut bacon, finely chopped*

15 g *(1 tbsp) extra virgin olive oil*

Prep time: 15 min
Cooking time: 15 min
Serves 2

1. Wrap oysters in aluminium foil, covering completely, and place on open fire or grill until foil turns golden brown, then flip. Approximately 3 minutes on each side. If using a conventional oven, open the oysters (but do not completely remove from the shell) before wrapping in foil, and cook for approximately 5 minutes on each side.

2. Place the leaves and stems of the swiss chard, the queso fresco, olive oil, and chopped bacon into a pan on medium-high heat until a crust layer forms at the bottom of the pan. Do not stir. Approximately 3 minutes.

3. Remove the top shells of the cooked oysters, and loosen oysters from their shells with a small knife.

4. Place oysters on a plate.

5. Spoon swiss chard and cheese crust atop each oyster.

JAIR TÉLLEZ
LAJA, VALLE DE GUADALUPE
32.05824 ° N, 116.59397 ° W

Jair Téllez tried really hard not to get into the food business, but he found himself a
chef anyway. While he now spends most of his time at his acclaimed second restaurant,
MeroToro, in Mexico City, Téllez earned his stripes and esteem in Baja at his first
restaurant, Laja. Opened in 2001 and set against the backdrop of the idyllic vineyards,
barns, and roaming horses of Valle de Guadalupe, Laja takes its inspiration from
the local-first ethos of Northern California cuisine. With deft execution and a keen
awareness of his restaurants' contexts, Téllez talks regional differences and which trends
he would like to see snuffed.

WHEN DID YOU FIRST OPEN LAJA?
I opened Laja in July 2001—so, 14 years ago. It
feels like something that was never going to happen
or wouldn't work out, but it did. And when things
defy that kind of improbability and happen for
inexplicable reasons, they have a certain sexiness to
them. That's pretty much what this place is to me.
It's emotional.

WHAT DO YOU MEAN BY THAT?
If there's no emotional connection, then we don't have
art. At our restaurant, we don't have sexy hostesses or
square plates. Nor do we plate dishes that seem like
a squirrel brought them in from the countryside. It's
about flavor, and it's about emotion. More than half
the staff has been here since day one. Some of them
were here planting stuff with me when they were
just kids. It really is a story about people with a great
excuse to make great food.

*THE RESTAURANT SITS IN THE MIDDLE
OF A VINEYARD AND IS SURROUNDED BY
VEGETABLES AND GRAPES. HOW DOES THAT
INFLUENCE THE RESTAURANT?*
For better or worse, people have compared us to
the French Laundry. And as inspiring as that is, we
have very different conditions and a very different
approach. We want to do what we want to do here;
that's the backbone of Laja. In the past, what we
wanted didn't match up with what customers wanted,
so we endured that. But now Valle is more in tune
with what we do, which is great.

*HAVE THE CUSTOMERS CHANGED OVER THE
LAST 14 YEARS?*
Valle has changed a lot. At the beginning, we had
more people from Tijuana and then we had Southern
Californians who wanted to get a cheaper version
of the Napa experience. Then the recession hit, and

Tijuana went through a period of insecurity. People
stopped coming here.

*DID THAT CHANGE THE KIND OF FOOD
YOU SERVED?*
We stopped having the kind of customers from
Southern California who expected chips and salsa,
and we started having well-informed—or at least
better informed, curious, better-educated—younger
Americans coming in. There were fewer people
coming in, but it was actually great. During those
years, more people from Central Mexico were coming
to Valle, too. Now we get both: people from Central
Mexico, along with more and more people from
Southern California.

*WHAT WAS IT LIKE WHEN YOU FIRST
OPENED LAJA?*
I was so nervous. I remember the first day we just
opened the door and nobody came. We said, "Okay,
maybe there's an explanation." So we got a piece of
wood and painted a sign that said we were open.
Thursday, nobody came. Friday, nobody came. And
then, Saturday, somebody came. We thought, "Okay,
great, let's do this."

It was a middle-aged couple with their daughter. I
gave them the menu. I remember looking at them
and thinking, "Fuck, maybe I should just start
making *chilaquiles*. This old French stuff I have
on the menu—ratatouille, carrot soup, fish with
herbs—is not going to work out." From there on out,
it luckily has always been enough to pay people and
keep going.

*HOW DID YOU DECIDE TO GET INTO THE
RESTAURANT BUSINESS?*
I tried not to. I went to law school for three years and
tried that. I'm an anthropologist, actually. Even then,

I just couldn't avoid being drawn into restaurants. I worked in restaurants when I was 13 and 15 years old, during summers and weekends. I liked it, but I also tried not doing it, and that didn't work out.

HOW HAS YOUR COOKING EVOLVED SINCE YOU OPENED THE RESTAURANT?

I always wanted to concentrate more on flavor and quality. I started with French food. Then there was some Italian, which I identified with because the Italian language of food is about treating great ingredients very simply and with a lot of integrity. Northern California's also inspired me.

One thing I will never compromise is quality. We didn't serve tables larger than six, and even now, I won't do an event for 30 people. How come? Because that might mess with quality, and maybe give off the impression that things here aren't done right. I want to be crazy about quality.

But it's a constant quest for identity. And I understand that it's totally uncool to talk about identity in an industry where people are expected to have a good time.

YOU'RE FROM TIJUANA, RIGHT?

I am from Tijuana, but I was not born in Tijuana. That's very Tijuana, because Tijuana kind of gets you. I was born in Sonora, but I moved to Tijuana when I was two years old. We moved for political reasons. My father was exiled from Sonora. He was a student leader. We were supposed to go back to Sonora and we never did, so we stayed in Tijuana, which again is very Tijuana. People in Tijuana just end up staying there.

DID YOU ENJOY GROWING UP THERE?

Yes, I'm very much a border person. I have the craftiness, irreverence, and personality of being from the border.

AT YOUR RESTAURANT MEROTORO IN MEXICO CITY, THERE'S DEFINITELY SOME BAJA INFLUENCE.

Yes, with ingredients and the approach. But there's also a total disregard of any obligation to put something "Mexican" on my dishes.

WHAT DO YOU MEAN BY THAT?

I'm not carrying the pyramid on my back. If I do something that has chiles, okay. If it doesn't have chiles, then I don't give a shit.

IS BAJA CUISINE NOT TYPICAL MEXICAN EATING?

It shouldn't be. I don't want to be insensitive, but how can I put it? These days, I see more and more homogenization of food in Baja that's trying to be more "Mexican." I love the richness of the Mesoamerican cultures, but it's not ours.

WHAT IS BAJA CUISINE THEN?

First of all, Baja cuisine is an attitude; you constantly question yourself. And if the answer happens to be a tamal, great. We're still figuring it out. That's why it's so magical. But there's this whole push towards having an easy answer to your identity, because it's scary not to, even though there's not an easy answer.

IS THAT UNIQUE TO BAJA?

We have an inside joke here. In San Francisco or Copenhagen, you can say, "You know what? I'm going to cook food that inspires me." Or, "I don't really know what I'm doing, but I'm doing what motivates me." Those would be great first words for a restaurant in Copenhagen. You can't do that in Mexico City, for example.

ARE THE CUSTOMERS AT YOUR RESTAURANT MEROTORO IN MEXICO CITY VERY DIFFERENT FROM WHAT YOU GET AT LAJA?

Yes. At Laja, they talk about the experience of dining at Laja. They're almost prepared to like it, because they drove from Tijuana, San Diego, or Ensenada. Which means they set aside between two, three, four, five, or six hours to eat there.

IT'S A DESTINATION RESTAURANT.

Emotionally, you're thinking about savoring the place and the experience. But we're very bad at doing gimmicks. We've probably lost some customers for it, but we'd rather do it our way.

YOU'RE NEAR THE COAST. DO YOU USE A LOT OF SEAFOOD?

We try to use what we can, which means we use seafood and lots of vegetables. The difficult part is the non-marine protein.

WHY?

Because it takes more to raise it properly. It's not wild

like the seafood, so it just takes more commitment from the producer and the consumer. It's easier to get that in the U.S.

HAVE YOU EVER THOUGHT ABOUT OPENING A RESTAURANT IN THE U.S.?
No, but I think of owning restaurants elsewhere.

WHY NOT THE U.S.?
I love the U.S., and I grew up with one foot on one side of the border and one in the other. But it doesn't move me that much to go into U.S., too. It's very competitive. It's much more exciting to think of doing restaurants in the rest of Latin America for me. For one, I have a cultural connection, and I also think every Latin American capital city should have a Mexican restaurant, because most of them currently have super bad ones. Plus, I have more fun when I go to South America. I love the U.S., but it's not as fun.

WHY IS IT SO HARD TO FIND GREAT MEXICAN FOOD OUTSIDE OF MEXICO?
The only thing, I guess, is what Rick Bayless does in Chicago. He's amazing. He's so much better at Mexican food than many Mexicans. Actually, I really think his restaurants best show what Mexican food means. Maybe it takes outside perspective to be able to see the big picture and put everything together.

WHAT DO YOU USUALLY SEE FROM OUTSIDERS THEN?
Have you ever noticed that whenever the center of the country makes food that becomes part of the national cuisine, it becomes saucy? The *machaca* [a type of dried meat] here is super dry. Then you get to Mexico City, and it's a stew. Everything's a stew suddenly. It's so weird: when you take food out of context here, it suddenly becomes saucy.

YOU SAID THIS BEFORE, BUT YOU DON'T USE VERY MANY CHILES IN YOUR FOOD. WHY NOT?
I use more chiles at MeroToro. At Laja, I don't use much. For one thing, there's a lot of wine here, and maybe 80 percent of the people coming here will drink wine. But most importantly, there aren't great chiles here. You find better chiles in Los Angeles than Ensenada.

WHAT DO YOU MEAN?
The flavors here have a very, very specific profile.

Vegetables tend to be very expressive because of the dryness and harshness of the environment. The beauty isn't just in the harshness; if it were, we'd get all of our food from the harsher Arizona desert. Here it happens in such an expressive way. Tomatoes here are very sweet. Herbs blow your mind. Some of them really kind of have a physical effect on your mouth and numb you. So when I cook, I take those things into account.

Food in Baja tends to be, flavor profile-wise, much more even. It doesn't have as many peaks and valleys. People here are coming from cities. They're wheeling and dealing, talking business. They sit down and they need to get food. It needs to stimulate them. You cannot really get away with doing a meal that's just okay, because people have traveled a long way to get here.

PRACTICALLY SPEAKING, WOULD YOU USE LESS OF CERTAIN INGREDIENTS HERE BECAUSE THE FLAVORS ARE STRONGER?
One of the challenges we're facing here is too much of certain flavors in cooking. Why is there aggressive smoke in everything in Baja? There's also too much rosemary. If you're in a larger environment, like in central Mexico, you don't see problems like that as quickly.

Here, I can tell you that right now there's too much smoke. And if we don't question it, we assume, "Yeah, it's too smoky, but that's Baja." What does that even mean? It's an easy way out, like saying in the Yucatán, let's put *achiote* and garlic on everything. We need to take these small things into account. The beauty of this place really is that it's fragile.

Tomato Water-Braised Eggplant

250 g *(half a medium-sized) creamy eggplant, such as a purple stripe eggplant*

24 g *(2 tbsp) extra virgin olive oil*

0.5 g *(1 sprig) thyme, stem removed*

15 g *(3 cloves) fresh garlic*

150 g *(1 small) tomatoes*

250 g *(1 cup) water*

1.5 g *(3 pinches) salt*

0.5 g *(1 pinch) black pepper*

1 g *(5-6 leaves) fresh basil*

Prep time: 20 min
Cooking time: 20 min
Serves 2

1. Put eggplant in a pan with olive oil on medium-high heat. Add a pinch of salt. Cook until eggplant turns golden brown, 6 to 7 minutes.

2. Add aromatics, including thyme and garlic. Let cook another 2 minutes to fully integrate flavors.

3. Add in the tomatoes and water to create a thin "tomato water." Do not add stock.

4. Move pan to an oven pre-heated to 350°F (175°C). Remove once sauce becomes firm, but still soft, approximately 12 minutes.

5. Plate the eggplant with the sauce, but leave out the larger pieces of tomatoes, thyme, and garlic.

6. Season with salt and pepper to taste. Garnish with fresh basil leaves.

Warm Rockfish, Squash, and Greens Salad

*110 g (6 long, 4 to 6-inch slices) rock fish,
       can be substituted for any lean fish*

48 g (4 tbsp) extra virgin olive oil

35 g (1 large) patty pan squash

40 g (1 small) shallot, finely diced

*90 g (3 cups) leafy greens (such as
       arugula, frisée, mizuna, kale)*

24 g (2 tbsp) sherry vinegar

0.5 g (1 pinch) sea salt

Prep time: 15 min
Cooking time: 10 min
Serves 2

1. Place the fish in a saucepan, skin-side down, with 2 tbsp of oil on medium-high heat until skin browns, approximately 3 to 4 minutes.

2. After the fish is removed, drain excess oil from the pan. Add the squash, diced shallot, and 1½ cup of leafy greens to heat for about 20 seconds, stirring often.

3. Add remaining 1½ cup of uncooked leafy greens into a bowl.

4. Add sherry vinegar and 2 tbsp of olive oil to greens already in the bowl. Combine with warm ingredients from the pan.

5. Season with salt and additional vinegar to taste. Optional: Garnish with fresh herbs, if available.

JAVIER PLASCENCIA

MISIÓN 19, TIJUANA
32.48431 ° N, 117.07304 ° W

When chef Javier Plascencia opened Misión 19 in Tijuana five years ago, he hoped it would help revitalize and re-energize a food city living in the shadow of the previous decade's violence. Born into a long line of restaurateurs and chefs there, Plascencia is unabashedly proud of his city—of its creative and plentiful food stalls, of its creative breweries, of its history—and gladly accepts his role as ambassador. It also helps that his food, steeped in an upbringing full of Italian cooking but focused on local ingredients and flavors, is infused with as much passion and personality as he brings to the table.

TELL US ABOUT YOUR RESTAURANT MISIÓN 19.

We opened Misión 19 five years ago when Tijuana was going through a rough time. We just wanted to do something for the city, and thought that if we opened a restaurant like Misión 19, we could get Tijuana back again on track and let people know that we were there and that nothing was going to take us down. We called it Misión 19 to pay tribute to the 18 missions from Cabo San Lucas up to Tijuana.

WHAT DID YOU DO BEFORE MISIÓN 19?

My parents opened a pizza place called Giuseppe's 47 years ago. That's really where I grew up. My family's been in the restaurant business for forever. I liked watching my parents work. They taught me a lot about how a restaurant should run and what passion and love for this business looks like.

When I graduated from cooking school, I came back to Tijuana with my dad and opened an Italian restaurant. At that time, my father had several pizza restaurants and worked with an Italian man who really taught him how people in Italy ate. Even though he was from Mexico and served Mexicans, he was very passionate about Italian food. We opened this Italian restaurant called Saverios 27 years ago, and I started out there. Great times.

WHAT WAS IT LIKE WORKING ALONGSIDE YOUR DAD?

It was an experience I will never forget. Ever since I was a little boy, I watched him work. The image I have of him is as a hard worker. I used to go with him to buy products, deal with clients, and create in the kitchen. He is super honest, friendly, and generous, always.

WHAT, IF ANYTHING, DID HE TEACH YOU?

Perseverance, most of all, because he lived through one of the two most hardcore recessions. There were ingredients like mozzarella from the U.S. that he was always worrying about—about the quality, the prices. He taught me that this business isn't about a lavish lifestyle. He was happy supporting his family and being able to educate them. It wasn't about money.

WHAT IS YOUR FATHER UP TO NOW?

He's still in the business—still opening restaurants, still in restaurants everyday. Now he's mostly taking care of guests and making sure the quality of food and service meets his standards.

HOW HAS THE RESTAURANT SCENE CHANGED IN TIJUANA OVER THE LAST DECADE?

Tijuana's always been a fun city and there have always been lots of restaurants—*taquerias*, lots of street food, bars, and plenty of places where tourists came to eat and drink. But Tijuana wasn't really serious about food. We had lots of Italian- and French-inspired restaurants—"continental," as they they used to call them. And then, of course, Tijuana had Chinese restaurants, which are a big part of our culture in Baja California because of Chinese immigrants that came to Baja California, first to Mexicali and eventually to Tijuana.

WHY COME HERE?

They came to work for the railroad, then stayed and built families here. I grew up eating Chinese food all my life. Next to my parents' pizzeria, there was a really good Chinese restaurant, where I would trade a pizza for egg rolls or chop suey.

WHEN DID THIS ALL BEGIN TO CHANGE?

I would say that Tijuana has always had interesting

food. But after the wave of violence that started around 2008, purveyors and cooks started to think more about the quality of the product and where it comes from.

This whole thing started because young, local Baja California chefs fresh out of school saw opportunity here. They saw something that, for many years, people didn't see: Baja California has an amazing array of fresh produce and local seafood. We have everything that a chef or restaurant would want or need to be 100 percent sustainable cooking Mexican Baja California cuisine.

WHAT DO YOU MEAN BY THAT?
We used to bring in salmon and swordfish from other places around the world. We even brought in mussels from New Zealand, and I thought, "What are we doing?" Everything started to change 10 or 12 years ago. Benito [Molina] and Jair [Téllez] and myself, along with other young guys coming from cooking school, helped revive what we now think of as food in Tijuana. We have so many amazing, talented young chefs doing *tacos* or *mariscos* in the street. The food truck scene is very happening here right now. And the quality of the food is amazing.

IS THE SAME TRUE OF TIJUANA'S BREWERIES?
Even the crappiest breweries in Tijuana are very, very good. And there's the wine, of course, from Valle de Guadalupe. But all these restaurants, like Misión 19, are part of the scene now and, as of about three years ago, people are coming to Tijuana as a food destination. Years ago, that's what we hoped for, and now it's starting to happen.

IT'S SO CLOSE TO THE U.S., AND THERE SEEMS TO BE LITTLE REASON WHY YOU CAN'T DRIVE OVER, HAVE LUNCH OR DINNER AND THEN DRIVE BACK. IS THAT HAPPENING YET?
It's starting to. More American tourists are coming, not just from California. We're getting more Mexican tourists, too. They used to just pass through Tijuana on the way to somewhere else, but now people make time to stay in Tijuana to eat, maybe spend the night. People from San Diego stopped coming for a while, but they're coming back again, too. I see it at my restaurants: probably 60 percent of my clientele is from California.

I mean, I do it. Sometimes I cross two times a day. The waiting time can be an issue, but it's getting better. On weekdays you make it over in as little as half an hour to 45 minutes.

TIJUANA HAS A REALLY INTERESTING CULINARY HISTORY.
A lot of people still don't know the Caesar salad was first created in Tijuana. It's one of the greatest recipes of all time, and there's a pretty cool story behind it. When I travel, and see Caesar salads on the menu, I always tell people, "Do you know this is a Mexican dish?" They always think it's Italian.

THE CAESAR SALAD ISN'T ITALIAN?
There are a couple of stories about it, but we did a lot of research and talked to a lot of people, and we think the best story starts with Caesar Cardini, the original owner of Caesar's Restaurant. They came from California to open a restaurant in Tijuana during a recession in the United States. The restaurant got a lot of tourists from California—movie stars and gamblers that came to the casino. People knew them from California. Livio Santini was a cook at Caesar's. He wanted to cross to America, but he stayed in Tijuana, and Cardini hired him as a cook.

One night after service, he was preparing this dish, and a client asked, "Hey, what are you eating?" He was eating salad with his hands and told her it was a recipe his mom used to cook for them in Italy. It was just eggs, stale bread, garlic, and lettuce from the farm. She asked, "Can you make it for our friends?" He did. They loved it and kept coming back for it. But it was ultimately created in Tijuana with Mexican ingredients.

HOW WOULD YOU CHARACTERIZE YOUR COOKING STYLE?
I started by cooking Italian. When I graduated cooking school, my father and I drove all over the Mediterranean. That was one of my first real food experiences, and it had a big impact on me. It was just me and my father driving, going to the markets, and tasting everything. It was crazy—eating cheese, bread, olives, olive oil. I really fell in love with Spanish and Italian cuisines after that trip.

HOW DID THAT AFFECT YOUR COOKING ONCE YOU RETURNED?
When I came back, I started cooking a lot of Italian

and Spanish food. Since my father already had started off the restaurant business with an Italian style, I followed that for a while. Then, I started discovering all the great ingredients here. I started buying local, and working with the local fish. It eventually hit me: I just said, "I'm Mexican. I'm here in Mexico. Why am I not cooking food influenced by that?" So, I started traveling around Mexico, talking to a lot of chefs and people, and then it all started to happen.

Now I've developed my own style with my local ingredients. I like strong flavors with lots of charcoal and mesquite. I love to cook outdoors. My dishes are very northern, I think. I like to play with textures and search for the freshest ingredients I can get. I have my own garden here, but we also buy from a lot of Tijuana locals. It's fun, and I'm pretty happy and excited about what's happening now. I think my food also tastes better and better because of the better ingredients I'm using.

IS THIS AN AREA OF MEXICO THAT HAS PARTICULARLY SPECIAL INGREDIENTS?

It does. A lot of chefs in Mexico look to Baja California to source ingredients. If you're in Mexico City, Guadalajara, or Monterrey, it's hard to get fresh seafood, for instance. A lot of it is flown from Baja California. Here, we have the opportunity to work very closely with producers. I make olive oil from olives we have here year-round, and I'm there with them pressing and tasting. We make our house wine with the same people. Then we get fresh seafood, and my guys let me know, "There's a ship coming with this type of fish." They will put it aside for me if it's really good.

IS THIS PHILOSOPHY SHIFT TRUE OF MEXICAN CUISINE IN GENERAL?

I think it's changing; it's definitely getting healthier and lighter. Mexican food has always been very colorful and we use a lot of vegetables and herbs. We have so many amazing ingredients that we can get very creative with our cuisine. But there's so much history in Mexican cuisine that we also need to be careful to preserve that and not go too crazy. If you're working with all the chiles that we have, or corn and *masa*, it's hard to get bored. That's why I like to change my menus so frequently; there's so much we can do here. And when I travel throughout Mexico, I see these young chefs doing amazing things, but it also tastes like Mexico. I love that.

Stuffed Zucchini

225 g (1 medium-sized) white onion

60 g (¼ cup) garlic, minced

24 g (2 tbsp) extra virgin olive oil

420 g (3 medium-sized) tomatoes

330 g (2 cups) fresh white corn, cut from cob

85 g (1 bunch) fresh epazote

13 g (1 tbsp) white vinegar

26 g (2 tbsp) white wine

1200 g (8 small) goldmine zucchini (can substitute with yellow summer squash)

240 g (1 cup) vegetable stock

0.5 g (1 pinch) salt

0.5 g (1 pinch) pepper

45 g (3 tbsp) extra virgin olive oil

80 g (2 cups) baby arugula

140 g (1 ½ cups) grated parmesan cheese

200 g (1 ½ cups) fresh cheese, such as queso fresco

4 zucchini blossoms

Prep time: 30 min
Cooking time: 15 min
Serves 8

1. Dice onions and garlic and cook in cast iron skillet over medium-high heat with olive oil until translucent.

2. Stir in tomatoes, corn, and epazote. Cook for 2 to 3 minutes.

3. Add vinegar and white wine. Let reduce for 2 to 3 minutes.

4. Add vegetable stock and two cubed zucchini to pan. Season with salt and pepper to taste, and continue cooking for about 5 minutes. Turn off heat and set aside.

5. Cut the remaining zucchini in half, lengthwise. Remove center of the zucchini with a spoon to create a cavity for the filling. Add filling to the center of the zucchini until it appears to overflow. Drizzle with olive oil and sprinkle with grated parmesan cheese.

6. Place stuffed zucchini under broiler on high heat until cheese begins to bubble and develops a thin crust. Garnish with fresh baby arugula and a few more drops of extra virgin olive oil.

7. Serve while hot. Garnish with zucchini blossoms.

The Original Caesar Salad

620 g *(1 head) romaine lettuce*

160 g *(3/4 cup) extra virgin olive oil*

15 g *(6 small) anchovy fillets (can substitute with oil-packed anchovies)*

5 g *(1 clove) garlic, crushed*

25 g *(1/4 cup) Parmesan cheese, grated*

5 g *(1 tsp) mustard*

5 g *(1 tsp) Worcestershire sauce*

50 g *(1 egg) yolk, coddled in shell*

30 g *(1 medium-sized) lime, juiced*

0.5 g *(a pinch) black pepper*

Prep time: 75 minutes
Assembly time: 15 minutes
Serves 2

1. Clean lettuce thoroughly, dry, and refrigerate until crisp, at least one hour.

2. In a wooden bowl combine olive oil, mustard, anchovies, garlic, and ¼ of the grated Parmesan. Whisk with a wooden paddle or spoon until a paste forms.

3. Once the coddled egg has completely cooled, crack the eggshell, and whisk yolk into existing paste until thoroughly blended. Set dressing aside.

4. Add whole romaine lettuce leaves and gently roll them into the dressing.

5. Season with the rest of the grated Parmesan cheese, fresh ground pepper, and salt to taste.

6. Optional: Top with a few garlic croutons.

TIJUANA

VALLE DE GUADALUPE

ENSENADA

EL ROSARIO

LORETO

LA PAZ

SAN JOSE DEL CA

CABO SAN LUCAS

Manta, Transpeninsular Highway Km 5
Cabo San Lucas, Baja California Sur, México.
22.89784 ° N, 109.86790 ° W

Blue Fish, Transpeninsular Highway Local 14A
San José del Cabo, Baja California Sur, México.
23.03834 ° N, 109.70924 ° W

Buffalo BBQ, Hotel La Posada, Calle Nueva Reforma
115 La Paz, Baja California Sur, México.
24.14695 ° N, 110.33802 ° W

Almejas Tatemadas, tinoalmejas_65@hotmail.com
Loreto, Baja California Sur, México.
26.00944 ° N, 111.33926 ° W

Mama Espinoza, Transpeninsular Highway Km 56
El Rosario, Baja California, México.
27.68607 ° N, 113.41166 ° W

Mariscos El Pizón, Av. Dr. Pedro Loyola
Ensenada, Baja California, México.
31.83894 ° N, 116.60688 ° W

Manzanilla, Recinto Portuario, Teniente Azueta #139
Ensenada, Baja California, México.
31.85944 ° N, 116.63256 ° W

La Guerrerense, Calle Primera esq. Alvarado, Centro
Ensenada, Baja California, México.
31.86145 ° N, 116.62309 ° W

Deckman's, Carretera Tecate-Ensenada Km. 85.5
Valle de Guadalupe, Baja California, México.
32.03560 ° N, 116.60163 ° W

Corazón de Tierra, Rancho San Marcos S/N, El Porvenir
Ensenada, Baja California, México.
32.03899 ° N, 116.65330 ° W

Laja, Carretera Ensenada-Tecate Km. 83
Valle de Guadalupe, Baja California, México.
32.05824 ° N, 116.59397 ° W

Misión 19, Misión San Javier 10643 2nd Floor
Tijuana, Baja California, México.
32.48431 ° N, 117.07304 ° W